A Tiger
Horseback

A Tiger on Horseback

The Experiences of a Trooper & Officer
of Rimington's Guides – the Tigers –
During the Anglo-Boer War
1899 – 1902

L. March Phillips

LEONAUR

A Tiger on Horseback: The Experiences of a Trooper & Officer of Rimington's Guides - the Tigers - During the Anglo-Boer War 1899 - 1902
by L. March Phillips

Originally published in 1902 under the title
With Rimington

Published by Leonaur Ltd

ISBN (10 digit): 1-84677-098-X (hardcover)
ISBN (13 digit): 978-1-84677-098-2 (hardcover)

ISBN (10 digit): 1-84677-087-4 (softcover)
ISBN (13 digit): 978-1-84677-087-6 (softcover)

http://www.leonaur.com

Publisher's Notes

In the interests of authenticity, the spellings, grammar and place names used have been retained from the original editions.

The opinions of the authors represent a view of events in which he was a participant related from his own perspective, as such the text is relevant as an historical document.

The views expressed in this book are not necessarily those of the publisher.

Contents

DEDICATION

This book is dedicated to the memory of my friend Lieutenant Gustavus Coulson, D.S.O., of the King's Own Scottish Borderers, who fell at Lambrechtfontein on May 19, 1901.

The Colonel in command writes that in that action Lieutenant Coulson rallied some men and saved a gun from falling into the enemy's hands. He lost his life in bringing off a wounded man from under the enemy's fire. For this deed, the last of many deeds as brave, he was recommended for the Victoria Cross.

I knew him from his childhood, and on the march from Lindley to Pretoria, and thence far south to Basutoland, we often rode together, and talked of West Country sport and his Devonshire home and faces that we both knew and loved there.

A keen soldier, a cheery comrade, and a brave and kindly English gentleman, he stands, it seems to me, the very type of those gallant boys who in this South African war have died for England.

PREFACE

These letters were written without any idea of publication, and it was not until I had been home some months that suggestions from one or two sources caused me to think of printing them. They appear much as they were written, except that sometimes several letters dealing with the same event have been thrown into one; and occasionally a few words have been added to fill up gaps. In no case have I been wise after the event, or put in prophecies which had already come off.

The parts in inverted commas are extracts from notebooks which I used to carry about in my pocket, and these passages I have left just as they were jotted down, thinking that such snap-shots of passing scenes might have an interest of their own.

It is unlucky from a descriptive point of view that the big actions and fine effects should all have occurred during the first part of the war, leaving the dulness and monotony for the later stages. During the last six months of my service it was not my chance to see any important action, though slight skirmishing was constant, and I find therefore nothing in the later letters of a very exciting nature.

Such as they are, however, these letters contain a quite faithful account of things that happened under my own eyes throughout the chief stages of the western campaign. During the early part of the war many things happened that were splendid to see and that it gave me great pleasure to write about. During the later stages nothing particularly splendid occurred, though the patience and endurance of our men were in their way fine; but some things happened which were, as we say, regrettable; and these things also are in their turn briefly described.

L.M.P.

15 Bury Street,
St. James's,
S. W.

Orange River Camp
Orange River, November 18, 1899

ORANGE RIVER CAMP
Orange River, November 18, 1899

The sun is just rising on Orange River Camp. Our tents are pitched on the slopes of white sand, soft and deep, into which you sink at every step, that stretch down to the river, dotted with a few scraggy thorn-trees. There are men round me, sleeping about on the sand, rolled in their dark brown blankets, like corpses laid out, covered from head to foot, with the tight folds drawn over their feet and over their heads. A few bestir themselves, roll, and stretch, and draw back the covering from their sleepy, dusty faces. The first sunbeams begin to creep along the ground and turn the cold sand yellow.

I am beginning this letter in the shade of a mimosa. The whole scene reminds me very much of Egypt; and you might easily believe that you were sitting on the banks of the Nile somewhere between the first and second cataract. There are the same white, sandy banks, the same narrow fringe of verdure on each side, the same bareness and treelessness of the surrounding landscape, the same sunscorched, stony hillocks; in fact, the whole look of the place is almost identical. The river, slow and muddy, is a smaller Nile; there only wants the long snout and heavy, slug-like form of an old crocodile on the spit of sand in the middle to make the likeness complete. And over all the big arch of the pure sky is just the same too.

Our camp grows larger and rapidly accumulates, like water behind a dam, as reinforcements muster for the at-.

tack. Methuen commands. We must be about 8000 strong now, and are expecting almost hourly the order to advance. Below us De Aar hums like a hive. From a deserted little wayside junction, such as I knew it first, it has blossomed suddenly into a huge depôt of all kinds of stores, provisions, fodder, ammunition, and all sorts of material for an important campaign. Trains keep steaming up with more supplies or trucks crowded with khaki-clad soldiers, or guns, khaki painted too, and the huge artillery horses that the Colonials admire so prodigiously. Life is at high pressure. Men talk sharp and quick, and come to the point at once. Foreheads are knit and lips set with attention. Every one you see walks fast, or, if riding, canters. There is no noise or confusion, but all is strenuous, rapid preparation.

Do you know Colonials? In my eight months of mining life at Johannesburg I got to know them well. England has not got the type. The Western States of America have it. They are men brought up free of caste and free of class. When you come among Colonials, forget your birth and breeding, your ancestral acres and big income, and all those things which carry such weight in England. No forelocks are pulled for them here; they count for nothing. Are you wide-awake, sharp, and shrewd, plucky; can you lead? Then go up higher. Are you less of these things? Then go down lower. But always among these men it is a position simply of what you are in yourself. Man to man they judge you there as you stand in your boots; nor is it very difficult, officer or trooper, or whatever you are, to read in their blunt manners what their judgment is. It is lucky for our corps that it has in its leader a man after its own heart; a man who, though an Imperial officer, cares very little for discipline or etiquette for their own sakes; who does not automatically assert the authority of his office, but talks face to face with his men, and asserts rather the authority of his own will and force of character. They are much more ready to knock

14

under to the man than they would be to the mere officer. In his case they feel that the leader by office and the leader by nature are united, and that is just what they want.

There are Colonials out here, as one has already come to see, of two tolerably distinct types. These you may roughly distinguish as the money-making Colonials and the working Colonials. The money-making lot flourish to some extent in Kimberley, but most of all in Johannesburg. You are soon able to recognise his points and identify him at a distance. He is a little too neatly dressed and his watch-chain is a little too much of a certainty. His manner is excessively glib and fluent, yet he has a trick of furtively glancing round while he talks, as if fearful of being overheard. For the same reason he speaks in low tones. He must often be discussing indifferent topics, but he always looks as if he were hatching a swindle. There is also a curious look of waxworks about his over-washed hands.

This is the type that you would probably notice most. The Stock Exchange of Johannesburg is their hatching-place and hot-bed; but from there they overflow freely among the seaside towns, and are usually to be found in the big hotels and the places you would be most likely to go to. Cape Town at the present moment is flooded with them. But these are only the mere froth of the South African Colonial breed. The real mass and body of them consists (besides tradesmen, &c., of towns) of the miners of the Rand, and, more intrinsically still, of the working men and the farmers of English breed all over the Colony. It is from these that the fighting men in this quarrel are drawn. It is from these that our corps, for instance, has been by the Major individually and carefully recruited; and I don't think you could wish for better material, or that a body of keener, more loyal, and more efficient men could easily be brought together.

Many of them are veterans, and have taken part in some

15

of the numerous African campaigns—Zulu, Basuto, Kaffir, Boer, or Matabele. They are darkly sunburnt; lean and wiry in figure; tall often, but never fat (you never see a fat Colonial), and they have the loose, careless seat on horseback, as if they were perfectly at home there. As scouts they have this advantage, that they not only know the country and the Dutch and Kaffir languages, but that they are accustomed, in the rough and varied colonial life, to looking after themselves and thinking for themselves, and trusting no one else to do it for them. You can see this self-reliance of theirs in their manner, in their gait and swagger and the way they walk, in the easy lift and fall of the carbines on their hips, the way they hold their heads and speak and look straight at you.

Your first march with such a band is an episode that impresses itself. We were called up a few days ago at dead of night from De Aar to relieve an outlying picket reported hard pressed. In great haste we saddled by moonlight, and in a long line went winding away past the artillery lines and the white, ghostly tents of the Yorkshires. The hills in the still, sparkling moonlight looked as if chiselled out of iron, and the veldt lay spread out all white and misty; but what one thought most of was the presence of these dark-faced, slouch-hatted irregulars, sitting free and easy in their saddles, with the light gleaming dully on revolver and carbine barrel. A fine thing is your first ride with a troop of fighting men.

Though called guides we are more properly scouts. Our strength is about a hundred and fifty. A ledger is kept, in which, opposite each man's name, is posted the part of the country familiar to him and through which he is competent to act as guide. These men are often detached, and most regiments seem to have one or two of ours with them. Sometimes a party is detached altogether and acts with another column, and there are always two or three with the staff. Besides acting as guides they are interpreters, and handy men generally. All these little subtractions reduce our main body to about a hundred, or a little less; and this main body, under Rimington himself, acts as scouts and ordinary fighting men. In fact, a true description of us would be "a corps of scouts supplying guides to the army."

One word about the country and I have done. What strikes one about all South African scenery, north and south, is the simplicity of it; so very few forms are employed, and they are employed over and over again. The constant recurrence of these few grave and simple features gives to the country a singularly childish look. Egyptian art, with its mechanical repetitions, unchanged and unvaried, has just the same character. Both are intensely pre-Raphaelite.

South Africa's only idea of a hill, for instance, is the pyramid. There are about three different kinds of pyramid, and these are reproduced again and again, as if they were kept all ready made in a box like toys. There is the simple kopje or cone, not to be distinguished at a little distance from the constructed pyramids of Egypt, just as regular and perfect. Then there is the truncated or flat-topped pyramid, used for making ranges; and finally the hollow-sided one, a very pretty and graceful variety, with curving sides drooping to the plain. These are all. Of course there are a few mistakes. Some of the hills are rather shakily turned out, and now and then a kopje has fallen away, as it were, in the making. But still the central idea, the type they all try for, is always perfectly clear. Moreover, they all are, or are meant to be, of exactly the same height.

Most strange and weird is this extraordinary regularity. It seems to mean something, to be arranged on some plan and for some humanly intelligible purpose. In the evenings and early mornings especially, when these oft-repeated shapes stand solemnly round the horizon, cut hard and blue against the sky like the mighty pylons and propylons of Egyptian

17

temples, the architectural character of the scenery and its definite meaning and purpose strike one most inevitably. So solemn and sad it looks; the endless plains bare and vacant, and the groups of pure cut battlements and towers. As if some colossals here inhabited at one time and built these remains among which we now creep ignorant of their true character. The scenery really needs such a race of Titans to match it. In these spaces we little fellows are lost.

Well, farewell. My next will be after some sort of a contest. There has been a touch or two; enough to show they are waiting for us. A corporal of ours was shot through the arm yesterday and struggled back to camp on another man's horse. The dark-soaked sleeve (war's colour for the first time of seeing!) was the object, you may guess, of particular attention.

BELMONT
Belmont Siding

BELMONT
Belmont Siding

It is to be called Belmont, I believe, from the little siding on the railway near which it was fought. On the other hand it may be called after the farm which it was fought on. Who decides these things? I have never had dealings with a battle in its callow and unbaptized days before, and it had never occurred to me that they did not come into the world ready christened. Will Methuen decide the point, or the war correspondents, or will they hold a cabinet council about it? Anyhow Belmont will do for the present.

What happened was the simplest thing in the world. The Boers took up their position in some *kopjes* in our line of march. The British infantry, without bothering to wait till the hills had been shelled, walked up and kicked the Boers out. There was no attempt at any plan or scheme of action at all; no beastly strategy, or tactics, or outlandish tricks of any sort; nothing but an honest, straightforward British march up to a row of waiting rifles. Our loss was about 250 killed and wounded. The Boer loss, though the extent of it is unknown, was probably comparatively slight, as they got away before our infantry came fairly into touch with them. The action is described as a victory, and so, in a sense, it is; but it is not the sort of victory we should like to have every day of the week. We carried the position, but they hit us hardest. On the whole, probably both sides are fairly satisfied, which must be rare in battles and is very gratifying.

Our mounted men, Guides, 9th Lancers, and a few

Mounted Infantry, marched out an hour before dawn. A line of *kopjes* stood up before us, rising out of the bare plain like islands out of the sea, and as we rounded the point and opened up the inner semicircle of hills, we could distinguish the white waggon tops of the Boer *laager* in a deep niche in the hillside, and see the men collecting and mounting and galloping about. By-and-by, as we advanced, there came a singing noise, and suddenly a great pillar of red dust shot up out of the ground a little to our left. "That's a most extraordinary thing," thinks I, deeply interested, "what land whale of these plains blows sand up in that fashion?" Then I saw several heads turned in that direction, and heard some one say something about a shell, and finally I succeeded in grasping, not without a thrill, the meaning of the phenomenon.

The infantry attack came off on the opposite side of the ridge from where we were, and we could see nothing of it. But we heard. As we drew alongside of the hills, suddenly there broke out a low, quickly uttered sound; dull reports so rapid as to make a rippling noise. The day was beautifully fine, still, and hot. There was no smoke or movement of any kind along the rocky hill crest, and yet the whole place was throbbing with Mausers. This was the first time that any of us had listened to modern rifle fire. It was delivered at our infantry, who on that side were closing with their enemy.

The fire did not last long, though in the short time it did terrible damage, and men of the Northumberlands and Grenadiers and Coldstreams were dropping fast as they clambered up the rocky hillside. But that brief burst of firing was the battle of Belmont. In that little space of time the position had been lost and won, and we had paid our price for it. During the march across the flat, as I have been told since, our loss was comparatively light; but when the climbing of the hill began, numbers of Boers who had been waiting ready poured in their fire. All along the ridge, from behind every rock and stone, the smokeless Mausers cracked (it was then the fire rose to that rippling noise we were listening to on the other side of the range), and the sleet of bullets, slanting down the hill, swept our fellows down by scores. But there was never any faltering. They had been told to take the hill. Two hundred and fifty stopped on the way through no fault of theirs. The rest went on and took it. That's the way our British infantry put a job through.

Soon, on our side, scattered bands of the enemy began to emerge from the *kopjes* and gallop north, whilst right up at the top of the valley their long convoy of waggons came into view, trekking away as hard as they could go, partly obscured by clouds of dust. We made some attempts to stop them, but our numbers were too few. Though defeated, they were not in any way demoralised, and the cool way in which they turned to meet us showed that they knew they were safe from the infantry, and did not fear our very weak cavalry. We did not venture to press the matter beyond long shots. Had we done so, it was evident we should have been cut up.

Various little incidents occurred. This one amused me at the moment. We had captured a herd of cattle from some niggers who had been sent by the Boers to drive them in, and I was conveying them to the rear. From a group of staff officers a boy came across the *veldt* to me, and presently I heard, as I was "shooing" on my bullocks, a very dejected voice exclaim, "How confoundedly disappointing." I looked round and saw a lad gazing ruefully at me, with a new revolver tied to a bright yellow lanyard ready in his hand. "I thought you were a Boer," he said, "and I was going to shoot you. I've got leave to shoot you," he added, as though he were in two minds about doing the job anyway. I looked at him for a long while in silence, there seemed nothing to say, and then, still ruefully, he rode away. This, you will understand, was right up our end of the valley, and I was driving cattle on to our ground, only I had a soft hat on.

We have plenty of youngsters like this; brave, no doubt, but thoughtless and quite careless about the dangerous qualities of the men they have to meet. "They'll live and learn," people say. They'll learn if they live, would perhaps be nearer the mark. The Boers, on the other hand, such as I have seen yet, are decidedly awkward-looking customers, crafty, but in deadly earnest, versed in veldt wars and knowing the country to an anthill. Looking from one to the other, I fear there are many mothers in England who'll go crying for their boys this campaign.

Later a troop of us penetrated into the deep recess among the hills where they had their laager. It seemed evident, from the number of waggons and the amount of clothing and stores left behind and littered in every direction, that the Boers had not expected to be shifted nearly so suddenly as they were. There were heaps of provisions, quantities of coffee tied up in small bags, sugar, rice, biltong, i.e. dried strips of flesh, a sort of bread biscuit much used by them on the march, and made at the farms, and other things. All were done up in small quantities in such a way that individual men could carry it. There were waggons loaded, or half loaded, with old chests and boxes, and many heaped about the ground. Most contained clothes, and the place was strewn in all directions with blankets, greatcoats, and garments of all sorts, colours, and sizes. I annexed a very excellent black mackintosh, quite new and splendidly lined with red; a very martial and imposing garment.

Diligent search was made for any paper or memoranda, which might show the plans or strength of the enemy, but all we found were the love-letters of the young Boers, of which there were vast numbers, extremely amusing. It never seems to have occurred to any of the writers that they could be going to get the worst of it. They seem to put the responsibility for the management of the whole campaign into the hands of the Deity. They are religious but practical.

"God will protect us. Here is a pound of coffee," is about what they all come to. It is the fashion to scoff at the calm way in which our enemies have appropriated the services of the Almighty, but all the same it shows a dangerous temper. People who believe they have formed this alliance have always been difficult to beat. You remember Macaulay's Puritan, with his "Bible in one hand and a two-edged sword in the other." The sword has given place to a Mauser now, but I am not sure that we are likely to benefit much by the change. As to the Bible, it is still very much in evidence. Not a single kit but contained one; usually the family one in old brown leather. Now it is an historical fact that Bible-reading adversaries are very awkward customers to tackle, and remembering that, I dislike these Bibles.

More practically important than love-letters and Bibles, we found also a lot of abandoned ammunition, shell and Mauser. Our ambulance parties were at work in the hills. Several Boers, as they fled, had been shot down near the laager. We found one, shot through the thigh, groaning very much, and carried him into the shade of a waggon, and did what we could for him. Meantime some of us had gathered bits of boxes and wood, and made a fire and boiled water. Tea-cups, coffee, sugar, and biscuits were found, and we made a splendid feast in the midst of the desolation. Horrid, you will say, to think of food among the dead and wounded. And yet that coffee certainly was very good. Somehow I believe the Boers understand roasting it better than we do.

Before going we collected all the ammunition and heaped it together and made a pile of wood round it which we set ablaze and then drew out into the plain and reined in and looked back. Never shall I forget the view. The hills, those hills the English infantry had carried so splendidly, were between us and the now setting sun, and though so close were almost black with clean-hacked edges against the sunset side of the sky. To eastward the endless grassy sea went whitening to the horizon, crossed in the distance with the horizontal lines of rich brown and yellow and pure blue, which at sunrise and sunset give such marvellous colouring to the veldt. The air here is exactly like the desert air, very exhilarating to breathe and giving to everything it touches that wonderful clearness and refinement which people who have been brought up in a damp climate and among smudged outlines so often mistake for hardness. Our great ammunition fire in the hollow of the hill burned merrily, and by-and-by a furious splutter of Mauser cartridges began, with every now and then the louder report of shells and great smoke balls hanging in the air. But sheer above all, above yellow veldt and ruined Boer *laager*, rose the hill, the position we had carried, grim and rigid against the sunset and all black. And, with the sudden sense of seeing that comes to one now and then, I stared at it for a while and said out loud "Belmont!" And in that aspect it remains photographed in my memory.

GRASPAN
November 26, 1899

A Boer Commando Unit

GRASPAN
November 26, 1899

We marched out from our Orange River Camp on November 22nd, and fought at Belmont on the 23rd. On the 24th we marched north again, and on the 25th (yesterday) fought another action at Graspan, or, as some call it, Enslin—there is still the difficulty about names. March a day and fight a day seems the rule so far.

At home, when you are criticising these actions of Methuen, you must always bear two facts in mind. First, we are bound to keep our line of communication, that is, the railway, open, and hold it as we advance. We can bring Kimberley no relief unless we can open and guard the railway, and so enable supplies to be poured into the town. Second, we are not strong enough, and above all not mobile enough, while holding the railway to attempt a wide flanking movement which might threaten the Boer retreat, or enable us to shell and attack from two sides at once. If we had anything like a decent force of mounted men I suppose we could do it, but with our handful to separate it from the main body would be to get it cut off. "Want of frigates" was to be found on Nelson's heart, as he said on some occasion, and I am sure by this time that "want of cavalry" must be written on poor Methuen's. So you must figure to yourself a small army, an army almost all infantry, and an army tied to the railway on this march; and if we bring off no brilliant strategy, but simply plod on and take hard knocks, well, what else, I ask, under the circumstances can we do?

Yesterday in the early morning we found ourselves emerging from some stony hills with a great plain before us about four miles wide, I should think, with an ugly-looking range of hills bounding it on the north and the railway running north and south on our left. This we had every reason to believe was the enemy's position; toll-gate No. 2 on the Kimberley road. We went on to reconnoitre. Rimington led us straight towards the hills in open order, and when we were somewhere about rifle range from them, we right turned and galloped in line along their front; but no gun or rifle spoke. When we reached the eastern point of the range, we turned it and rode on with the hills on our left; and now, with the Lancers a little farther out on our right, we offered too good a shot for the enemy to resist. They opened on us with, as I thought three, but others think two, guns, and put in some quick and well-directed shots, of which the first one or two fell short and the rest went screaming over our heads and fell among the Lancers.

One point of difference, I notice, so far as a short experience goes, between cavalry and infantry, which is all in favour of the cavalry; and that is, that when they get into fire the infantry go calmly on, while the much wiser cavalry generally run away. We retired from these guns, but when opposite the corner of the range the Lancers got on to some bad ground in front of us, and we had to halt a minute, which gave the Boer Long Tom an excellent chance of a few parting words with us. The first shell came along, making the mad noise they do, whooping and screaming to itself, and plunged into the ground with a loud snort only about thirty or forty yards off. The gunner, having got his range, was not long in sending down another, and when the white curl of smoke appeared lying again on the hillside, one guessed that the individual now on his way would prove a warmish customer. It burst with a most almighty crack, and I involuntarily bent down my head over

30

my horse's neck. "Right over your head," shouted the next man, in answer to my question as to where it burst.

If you are at all interested in "projectiles," you may care to hear that shrapnel is most effective when it bursts over, but a little short of, the object aimed at; the bullets, released by the bursting charge, continuing the line of flight of the shell, which is a downward slant. There is a rather anxious interval, of about ten or fifteen seconds generally after you see the smoke of the gun, and before anything else happens. Then comes the hollow boom of the report, and almost immediately afterwards the noise of the shell, growing rapidly from a whimper to a loud scream, with a sudden note of recognition at the end, as if it had caught sight of and were pouncing on you. It is a curious fact, however, that, in spite of the noise they make, you cannot in the least distinguish in which direction they are coming. You find yourself looking vaguely round, wondering where this yelling devil is going to ground, but till you see the great spurt of earth you have no idea where it will be. We came back across the plain, having more or less located the position and the guns. Rimington with one squadron got into a tight place among some *kopjes* on our right. The rifle fire was very hot, and at close range. The Major took up his orderly, whose horse was shot, on his own pony, and brought him off. For a moment the squadron came under cover of a hill, but they had to run the gauntlet of the Boer fire to get away. Rimington laughingly asked for a start as his pony was carrying double, and rode first out into the storm of bullets. Several men and horses were hit, but no men killed, and they were lucky in getting off as cheap as they did. We then drew back to a cattle kraal on the slope overlooking the plain, from which we watched the development of the infantry attack.

I usually carry a note-book and pencil in my pocket, partly to jot down any information one may pick up at farms from Kaffirs, &c., and partly to make notes in of the

31

things I see. Here is a note from the *kraal*.

"10 A.M.—There is a wide plain in front of me, four miles across, flat as the sea, and all along the farther side a line of *kopjes* and hills rising like reefs and detached islands out of it. You might think the plain was empty at first glance, but, if you look hard, you will see it crawling with little khaki-clad figures, dotted all over it; not packed anywhere, but sprinkled over the whole surface. They are steadily but very leisurely converging on the largest end hill of the opposite range. Meantime, from three or four spots along the sides of those hills, locks and puffs of white smoke float out, followed at long intervals by deep, sonorous reports; and if you look to the left a bit, where our naval guns are at work, you will see the Boer shells bursting close to or over them. The artillery duet goes on between the two, while still the infantry, unmolested as yet, crawls and crawls towards those hills."

This is our first sight of an infantry attack, and it doesn't impress me at first at all. Its cold-bloodedness, the absence of all excitement, make it so different from one's usual notions of a battle. It is really difficult to believe that those little, sauntering figures are "delivering an attack." They don't look a bit as if they were going to fight. The fact is, they have a long distance to cover before reaching the hills, and must go fairly slow. Accordingly, you see them strolling leisurely along as if nothing particular were happening; while the hills themselves, except for the occasional puffs of smoke, look; quite bare and empty; ridges of stone and rock, interspersed with grass tussocks, heaped up against the hot, blue sky.

But now, as they advance farther across the plain, the muffled, significant sound of the Mauser fire begins. The front of the attack is already so far across that it is impossible to see how they are faring from here; but it is evident that our shell fire, heavy though it has been, for all our guns have been in action some time now, has not turned the Boers out of their position. The big chunks of rock are an excellent defence against shrapnel, and behind them they lie, or down in the hollow of the hills, as we saw them earlier in the day, to be called up when the attack approached; and now, gathering along the crest, their fire quickens gradually from single shots to a roar. But it has no effect on that fatal sauntering! Of the men who leave this side nigh on two hundred will drop before they reach the other, but still, neither hurrying nor pausing, on they quietly stroll, giving one, in their uniform motion over that wide plain, a sense as of the force and implacability of some tidal movement. And, as you watch, the significance of it all grows on you, and you see that it is just its very cold-bloodedness and the absence of any dash and fury that makes the modern infantry attack such a supreme test of courage.

Of the details of the attack, when it came to the last charge, we could see nothing. The Naval Brigade, who had the hardest part of the position to take, lost terribly, but did the job in a way that every one says was perfectly splendid. It is said, however, that they made the mistake, in the scaling of the hill, of closing together, and so offering a more compact mass to the enemy's fire. We came on behind the infantry with our friends the Lancers, and passed through a gap in the range and on across some open ground and through a few more *kopjes* as fast as we could go. Then we came in sight of the enemy, and the same thing happened as at Belmont. A lot of horsemen, enough to have eaten us up, that were hanging about the rear of the Boer column, came wheeling out against us, and as we continued to approach, opened fire. Luckily there was good cover for our ponies behind some hillocks, and, leaving them there, we crawled out among the rocks and blazed at the Boers. But this was all we could do. We daren't attack. The only hope was guns, and it was a long and inexplicable time before any guns came up. By that time the Boer column was almost across the plain, winding its way in among the *kopjes* on the farther side, but the 15-pounders made some very pretty practice at the rear-guard, and considerably hastened their movements. The Boer retreat seems to have been conducted with much coolness and method. They ceased firing their big guns while the attack was still a good way distant, and limbered up and sent them on, the riflemen remaining till the attack was close upon them, and firing their last shots right in our infantry's faces, then rushing down to their horses and mounting and galloping off. No doubt, they exposed themselves a bit in doing this, but pumped and excited men can't be expected to shoot very straight, and I'm afraid their losses were light compared to ours. They have now retired, we presume, to the next range of kopjes, there to smoke their pipes and read their Bibles and await our coming. I suppose we shall be along tomorrow or next day.

MODDER RIVER
Modder River Camp, December 1, 1899

MODDER RIVER
Modder River Camp, December 1, 1899

We had a great old fight here two days ago, and suffered another crushing victory; but though I saw it all, I daresay you know more about the whole thing by this time than I do.

This is the Modder River, deep and still, just beneath my feet. It is a lovely, cloudless morning, and going to be a very hot day. I am writing my letter on the banks of the river in the shade of green trees and shrubs, with birds singing and twittering, and building their nests round me; it is spring-time here, you know, or early summer. Here and there, sauntering or sitting, are groups of our khaki soldiers enjoying mightily a good rest after the hard work, marching and fighting, of the last ten days. From the river-bed come voices calling and talking, sounds of laughing, and now and then a plunge. Heads bob about and splash in the mud-coloured water, and white figures run down the bank and stand a moment, poised for a plunge. Three stiff fights in seven days doesn't seem to have taken much of the spring out of them.

You would scarcely think it was the scene of a battle, and yet there are a few signs. If you look along the trees and bushes, you see here and there a bough splintered or a whole trunk shattered, as though it had been struck by lightning. A little lower down the river there is a shed of corrugated iron, which looks as if some one had been trying to turn it into a pepper-pot by punching it all over with

37

small holes. They run a score to the square foot, and are a mark of attention on the part of our guards, who, lying down over yonder in the plain, could plainly distinguish the light-coloured building and made a target of it. In many places the ground is ploughed up in a curious way, and all about in the dust lie oblong cylinders of metal, steel tubes with a brass band round one end. These would puzzle you. They are empty shell cases. The tops, as you see, have been blown off, which is done by the bursting charge timed by a fuse to ignite at a certain range, i.e., above and a little short of the object aimed at. The explosion of the bursting charge by the recoil, checks for an instant the flight of the shell, and this instant's check has the effect of releasing the bullets with which the case is filled. These fly forward with the original motion and impetus of the shell itself, spreading as they go. Horizontal fire is easy to find cover against, but these discharges from on high are much more difficult to evade. For instance, ant-hills are excellent cover against rifles, but none at all against these shells. It is shrapnel, as this kind of shell is called, that does the most mischief. The round bullets (200 to a caseful) lie scattered about in the dust, and mixed with them are very different little slender silvery missiles, quite pretty and delicate, like jewellers' ornaments. These are Lee-Metford bullets. You could pick up a pocketful in a short time.

The action itself was mainly an infantry one. Here are one or two jottings taken that day:—

"November 26th, 7.30 A.M.—We left camp, six miles south of Modder River, a little before daylight and marched north. The country is like what one imagines a North American prairie to be, a sea of whitish, coarse grass, with here and there a low clump of bushes (behind one of which we are halted as I write this). One can see a vast distance over the surface. Along the north horizon there is a ripple of small hills and *kopjes*, looking blue, with the white grass-land running up to them. It is a comparatively cool morning with a few light clouds in the sky and a pleasant breeze. On our left is the railway, and all along on our right, extending far in front and far behind, advances the army."

"We incline to the left near to the railway. The horrid, little, grey-bluish, armoured train crawls in front. It is dreadfully excited always in presence of the enemy, darting forward and then running back like a scorpion when you tease it with your stick-end. One can see by its agitation this morning that the enemy are not far off. Behind it comes a train of open trucks with the famous Naval Brigade, with their guns, search-light, &c. The river flows somewhere across the landscape yonder in the plains. One cannot see it, but a few belts of bushes indicate its course. It is just that awkward moment before one gets touch of the enemy. They, no doubt, can see us (I wonder how they like the look of us), but we cannot see them. They must be somewhere along the river among those bushes, and probably in trenches. But where does their main strength lie? where are their guns? There goes fire, away on the right (probably at the Lancers, who are the right flankers); the dull short discharge of Mausers. The train moves forward a hundred yards, but as yet the men keep their places, clustered in the trucks. Two officers standing on a carriage roof watch with a telescope the distant fire. It has now ceased. A flag-wagger flutters his flag in eager question. Nothing moves on the plain save here and there a lonely prowling horseman, cantering on, or dismounted and peering through his glass. It was three minutes to eight when the first shot was fired. 'This will be a bit more history for the kiddies to learn,' yawns the next man to me, leaning idly over his pony."

"It is a half-hour later as the great guns begin their booming; that solemn, deep-toned sound like the striking of a great cathedral clock. We moved forward to the top of a rise overlooking the distant river and village."

"A dead level stretches below us to the river, marked by some bush tufts and the few roofs of Modder River village. The Naval Brigade have got their four guns in the plain just near the foot of our hill. They are hard at work now bombarding the enemy's big gun by the river. This, after a while, is almost silenced. Each time it speaks again the deadly naval guns are on to it. At last, when it does fire, it shows by its erratic aim that its best gunners are out of action."

"9.30.—The naval guns draw slowly closer to the river. Every shell bursts along the opposite bank where the enemy are. More to the right and nearer the river our field-batteries are pounding away as hard as they can load and fire. All the time the subdued rumble of Maxims and rifles goes on, like a rumble of cart-wheels over a stony road. Now it increases to one continuous roar, now slackens till the reports separate. Now, after one and a half hours, the fight seems to be concentrating towards the village opposite. A haze of smoke hangs over the place. The guns thunder. The enemy's Maxim-Nordenfelt goes rat-tat-tat a dozen times with immense rapidity. 'Come in,' says a Tommy of the Grenadiers who has come to our hill for orders; and indeed it sounds exactly like some one knocking at a street door. Now the under-current of rifle fire becomes horrible in its rapidity. Can anything in that hell down there be left alive? Suddenly their plucky big gun opens again and sends several well-directed shells among our batteries. The naval guns turn their attention to it immediately. You can see the little, quick glints of fire low along the ground at each discharge, and then the bursting shell just over the big gun on the river-bank."

"10 A.M.—Both sides are sticking to the business desperately. The rattle of rifle-fire is one low roar. The air shudders and vibrates under it. Now the naval guns draw towards the river again; so do the rest of our batteries. Things can't stand at this tension. The big gun speaks again, but wildly; its shell bursts far out on the plain."

"10.30.—The aspect of the place is now awful. The breeze has died a little and the smoke hangs more. It is enveloped in a haze of yellow and blue vapour, partly from bursting shell and partly firing guns. Those volumes of smoke, with gleams of fire every now and then, make it look like some busy manufacturing town, and the blows and throbs with which the place resounds convey the same idea."

"11 A.M.—The fight is dogged as ever but slower. There are cessations of firing altogether, and it is comparatively slow when continued. The stubbornness of the enemies' resistance to our attack and to the fearful shelling they have had is calling forth expressions of astonishment and admiration from the onlooking officers on the hill."

"As the circle narrowed and our attack concentrated on the village and bridge, we all thought that the end was coming, and, on a lull of the firing about 11.30 the Major even exclaimed, 'There, I think that's the end, and I can only say thank God for it.' But he was wrong. He had scarcely said it when that indomitable heavy gun of theirs, re-supplied with gunners, began again; again the Naval guns, on a tested range, crack their shrapnel right in its face; the batteries all open and soon the whole orchestra is thundering again. That dreadful muttering, the *rub-a-dub, a-dub-a-dub, a-dub-a-dub* (say it as fast as you can) of the rifles keeps on; through all the noise of fire, the sharp, quick bark of the Boer Maxim-Nordenfelt sounds at intervals and the mingled smoke and dust lies in a haze along the river."

It was, all through, almost entirely an infantry action, but about the middle of the day we were sent down to the river on the Boer right, as parties of the enemy were thought to be breaking away in that direction. And here, I am sorry to say, poor Parker who had served in the Greek-Turkish war, and used to beguile our long night marches with stories of the Thessalian hills and the courage of the Turks, was hit, it is feared mortally. The fight itself continued with intermissions all day, and even in the evening, though parts of the Boer position had been captured and many of them had fled, there were some who still made good their defence, holding out in places of vantage with the greatest obstinacy. These took advantage of the night to escape, and it was not till next morning that we had the place in our possession. The Boers themselves, as we are told by people here, thought the position impregnable. Certainly it was very strong. The river has cut a channel or groove thirty feet deep in the ground; the edges, sharp and distinct, so that men can lie on the slant and look out across the plain. A big loop in the river is subtended by a line of trenches and rifle-pits hastily dug (they only decided twenty-four hours before the attack to defend the position; this by Cronjé's advice, who had just come south from Mafeking, the others were for retiring to the next range of hills), from which the whole advance of our infantry across the level is commanded. "We," as the soldiers explained to me, "could see nothing in our front but a lot of little heads popping up to fire and then popping down again." These shelters, a long line of them, are littered thick with empty cartridge cases, hundreds in each; one thinks involuntarily of grouse-driving. Bodies, still unburied, lay about when I was there. Such odours! such sights! The unimaginable things that the force of shot and shell can do to poor, soft, human flesh. I saw soldiers who had helped to do the work turn from those trenches shaking.

THE FOUR POINT SEVEN
Modder River Camp, December 1899

HE IS OUT ON ACTIVE SERVICE,
WIPING SOMETHING OFF A SLATE

Kipling

THE FOUR POINT SEVEN
Modder River Camp, December 1899

A few days ago we welcomed a distinguished stranger here in the shape of a long 4.7 naval gun. They set him up in the road just outside the station, with his flat-hatted sailors in zealous attendance, where he held a day-long levée. The gun is a remarkable object among the rest of our artillery. Its barrel, immensely long but very slender, has a well-bred, aristocratic look compared with the thick noses of our field-guns. It drives its forty-five pound shell about seven miles, and shoots, I am told, with perfect accuracy. It is an enlarged edition of the beautiful little twelve-pounders which we have hitherto been using, and which exceed the range of our fifteen-pounder field-guns by about a half. Why should naval guns be so vastly superior to land ones?

I interviewed the sailors on the accomplishments of the new-comer, and on the effects especially of lyddite, about which we hear so much. One must allow for a little friendly exaggeration, but if the mixture of truth is in any decent proportion, I should say that spades to bury dead Boers with are all the weapons that the rest of us will require in future. The gun uses shrapnel as well, but relies for its main effects on lyddite. As for this horrible contrivance, all I can say is that the Geneva Conference ought to interdict it. The effects of the explosion of a lyddite shell are as follows:—Any one within 50 yards is obliterated, blown clean away. From 50 to 100 yards they are killed by the force of the concussion of the air. From 100 to 150 yards they are killed by the fumes or poisonous gases which the shell exhales. From 150 to 200 they are not killed, but knocked senseless, and their skin is turned to a brilliant green colour. From 200 to 250 they are so dazed and stupefied as to be incapable of action, and, generally speaking, after that any one in the district or neighbourhood of the shock is "never the same man again." This is no mere rumour, for I have it direct from the naval gunners themselves.

This morning, well before light, we took out our gentleman, dragged by an immense string of oxen, to introduce him to his future victims and whet his appetite by a taste. The Boer position lies some six miles to the north of the river. The most conspicuous feature of it is a hill projecting towards us like a ship's ram and dipping sharply to the plain. Magersfontein, they call it. The railway going north leaves it to the right, but other hills and *kopjes* carry on the position westward across the railway, barring an advance. It is evident that we shall have to take the place in front, as we are not strong enough nor mobile enough to go round.

We have a few reinforcements, notably the Highland Brigade, also the 12th Lancers under Airlie, and some Horse Artillery pop-guns.

There is a good deal of bush on the plain, especially to the right of the steep hill, where it is quite thick. During the last week we have been poking about in this a good deal, approaching the hill now on this side, now on that, under cover of the scrub, examining and searching, but with very little result. They keep themselves well hidden. The hills look untenanted except that now and then we have seen parties of Boers wending their way in between the *kopjes* and driving in herds of cattle.

In the thick bush on the eastern plain, as we lay one morning at daybreak, we could hear the shouts of men and catch glimpses of them here and there riding about and urging their cattle on. Some passed not far from where we lay crouched (we had left our ponies on the outskirts of the bush). It seemed funny to watch them riding to and fro, unconscious of our presence and calling to each other. It reminded me of some boy's game of hide-and-seek or Tom Tiddler's ground. We have had two or three casualties, and lost two prisoners, and we have bagged several of them. The army is resting.

Well, this morning, as I was saying, we take our Long Tom (Joey, as he is now called, out of compliment to Chamberlain) out for a shot. Here is a note about it:—

"4.30 A.M.—Our little groups of horse, in threes and fours, are clustered behind bushes. There is a whispered consultation round our large gun and his nose slowly rises. The jerk of the lanyard is followed by a frightful explosion and then comes the soaring noise of the flying shell and the red spark and column of dust on the kopje. The range has been well judged, for the first shot falls with beautiful accuracy just on the hill where they are supposed to be.

"It is worth getting up at this time to enjoy the delicious, pure, and fresh air. The glow of sunrise is in the sky, but not yet the sun. There are some long streaks and films of rosy cloud along the east. Already, after five shots, the whole kopje is enveloped in dust and reddish smoke from the bursting lyddite, but elsewhere between us and the sunrise the hills are a perfect dark blue, pure blocks of the colour. The Lancers on their horses show black against the sky as they canter, scattering through the underwood with graceful slanting lances. At slow deliberate intervals the long gun tolls. Dead silence is the only reply. The sun rises and glares on the rocky hills. Not a living thing is to be seen."

49

MAGERSFONTEIN

Modder River Camp, December 13, 1899

MAGERSFONTEIN
Modder River Camp, December 13, 1899

When we were camped a day's march south of this, two Boers brought in a wounded man of ours in a Cape cart. "You will never get to Kimberley," they said to us. "It will take better men than you to stop us," said we. "Not a bit of it," said they, and off they drove. As it turns out, they were nearer the mark than we were.

While I write this, early on the morning of the 13th, you at home may just be reading in the papers the accounts of our last two days' disastrous fighting. It was a defeat, but yet it was a defeat which was not felt nor realised by the bulk of the army. It was a blow that fell entirely on one brigade, and the greater part of our force was still awaiting the order to advance, and expecting to engage the enemy when already the attack, unknown to us, had been delivered and repulsed.

Last Sunday, December 10th, about 2 P.M., we moved out of camp northward towards the point of the big hill, that, like a cape, juts south into the plain. With all our guns ranged about the point of the hill, we then proceeded to thrash and batter it with shell-fire. No gun-fire that we have had as yet has approached this for rapidity. The batteries roared ceaselessly from the plain; the big 4.7 lifting up its voice from a little in the rear high above the din. The day was cloudy, and rain fell at intervals, but towards the evening it cleared. My troop was on the extreme left front, on the west side of the hill, and we had a fine view of the effect as the shells burst one after another, or sometimes three or four together, all along the hill flank, up on the crest, or in the plain along the base.

> "5 P.M.—The hill is all one heavy dull hue in the sombre evening light, and against it the sharp glints of fire as the shrapnel bursts, and the round puff-balls of white smoke show vividly. Every now and then a great curtain of murky vapour goes up to show where the old lyddite-slinger in the rear is depositing his contributions. We had three field-batteries engaged, the naval twelve-pounders, Joey, and the pop-guns; about thirty guns altogether."

We slept that night by the side of the railway, tethering our horses to the wire fence that runs down it. Rain fell heavily all night. Most of us had no blankets, and we lay bundled up, shivering under our greatcoats on the sopping ground. Unable to sleep well, I heard, just about or before dawn, a distant drumming, like the noise of rain on the window, but recognised immediately as distant rifle-fire. Morning broke, cheerless and wet. I asked if any one had heard firing during the night, but no one near me had. Shivering and breakfastless, save for a morsel of biscuit and a sip of muddy water, we saddle our dripping horses and fall in. A Tommy sitting in the ditch, the picture of misery; cold, and hungry, with the rain trickling from his sodden helmet on to his face; breaks into a hymn, of which the first verse runs:—

There is a happy land
Far, far away,
Where they get ham and eggs
Three times a day.

I find myself dwelling on the words as we move off. Can there be such a land? Can there be so blessed a place?

We reach the ganger's hut, and the light spreads and rests on the hills. Immediately we are deafened by a shattering report close behind us, and starting round, find the long nose of Joey projecting almost over our heads, while the scream of the shell dies away in the distance as it speeds towards the Boer hill. One of the naval officers gives me a first hint of the truth. There has certainly been an attack, he says, but he fears unsuccessful.

We took the matter up, then, where we left off yesterday, all our batteries coming into action and shelling the hills most furiously. The enemy replied with three guns only, but so well placed were they that we found it impossible to silence them. While our fire was concentrated on to any one of them, it would remain silent, but, after a short interval, would always begin again, to the rage of our gunners. There is especially a big gun of theirs in a fold of the hill just at the crest, between which and "Joey" exist terms of mortal defiance. Nothing else it appears can touch either of them; so while the lesser cannonade rages in the middle, these two lordly creatures have a duel of their own and exchange the compliments of the season with great dignity and deliberation over the others' heads. It has gone all in favour of "Joey" while I was watching, the Boer gun being rather erratic and most of its shells falling short. It made one good shot just in front of us, and it was really comic to see how "Joey," who had been looking for other adversaries for the moment, came swinging round at the voice of his dearest foe. The explosion of the big gun almost knocks one backwards, and I feel the sudden pressure on my ears of the concussion.

Later in the day "Joey" and I got quite thick. There is a double kopje, detached from the main Boer position on our side, known as the Dumbell Kopje. From our left-front place we could see a lot of Boers clustered under the hill, pasted, like swarming bees, up against the lee of it, while the naval gun's shells—for he evidently had a nonchalant idea that there was some one about there—went flying overhead and bursting beyond. This was very irritating to watch, and I was glad to be sent back to "whisper a word in his ear." Making a hasty sketch of the hill, I galloped back and presented it to the captain with explanation, and had the satisfaction of seeing 300 yards knocked off "Joey's" next shot, which was, I should judge, a very hot one. "Stay and have some grub," said the jolly naval captain. We sat on the ground eating and drinking, while "Joey" peppered the Dutchmen.

As for the fight itself, people seem inclined to make a great mystery about it and talk about "the difficulty of getting at the truth;" but I don't see myself where the mystery comes in. What happened was this. The Highland Brigade (Black Watch, Seaforths, Argyle and Sutherlands, and Highland Light Infantry) was told off for the night attack and marched before light to the hill. The night was very dark and heavy rain falling. The ground was rough, stony, and rocky, with a good deal of low scrub, bushes, and thorn trees, very difficult to get through at night. The difficulty of moving masses of men with any accuracy in the dark is extreme, and to keep them together at all it was necessary for them to advance in a compact body. In quarter column, therefore, the Brigade advanced and approached the foot of the hill. I have noticed several times that when you get rather close to the hill the rise comes to look more gradual and the ridge itself does not stand up in the abrupt and salient way that it does from a distance. Whether it was this, or simply that the darkness of the night hid the outline, at any rate the column approached the hill and the trench which runs at the foot of the hill much too closely before the order to extend was given. When it was given it was too late. They were in the act of executing it when the volley came.

Of course an attack like this cannot be intended altogether as a surprise—that is, it cannot be pushed home as a surprise. You cannot march 4000 heavy-booted men through broken ground on a dark night without making plenty of noise over it; also the Boers must certainly have had pickets out, which would have moved in as we advanced and given the alarm. But had our fellows deployed at half a mile, or less, under cover of darkness, and then advanced in open order, the enemy could not have seen clearly enough to shoot with accuracy until they were fairly close, and I daresay the fire then would not have stopped their rush.

As it was, the fire came focussed on a mass of men, such a fire as I suppose has never been seen before, for not only was it a tremendous volley poured in at point-blank range, but it was a sustained volley; the rapid action of the magazines enabling the enemy to keep up an unintermittent hail of bullets on the English column. To advance under fire of this sort is altogether impossible. It is not a question of courage, but of the impossibility of a single man surviving. At the Modder fight our men advanced to a certain distance, but could get no nearer. They were forced to lie down and remain lying down. The fire of magazine rifles is such that, unless helped by guns or infinitely the stronger, the attackers have no chance of getting home. People will keep on talking as if courage did these things. What the devil's the use of the bravest man with half-a-dozen bullets through him? It is just as certain as anything can be that, if the Highlanders had "gone on," in two minutes not a man would have been left standing. Already in the brief instant that they stood, dazed by the fire, they lost between six and seven hundred men. The Black Watch was in front, and nineteen out of twenty-seven officers were swept down. You might as well talk of "going on" against a volcano in eruption.

I am writing this on the day after the action in my favourite lurking-place by the side of the river under the evergreens and big weeping willows that overhang the sluggish water. Our own small camp is close to the stream, and here every morning the Highlanders are in the habit of turning up, usually with much laughing and shouting, to bathing parade. There is no laughing this morning, only sad, sullen faces, silence and downcast looks. Still they are glad to talk of it. A few come under the shade of my tree, and sit about and tell me the little bit that each saw or heard. You only get a general impression of chaos. Some tried to push on, some tried to extend, some lay down, and some ran back out of close range and took up such cover as they could get. This was, luckily, pretty good, there being a lot of bush and rocks about, and here they gradually crawled together and got into some sort of order, and kept up a counter fire at the Boer position. The Brigade, however, had been badly shaken, and as hour after hour passed all through the blazing day, and they were kept lying there under the fire of an entrenched enemy, exhausted and parched with thirst, their patience gradually failed, and they made another rush back, but were rallied and led up again to where the Mausers might play on them. They were not allowed to retire till after five, when all the troops were withdrawn—that is, until they had been shot over at close range for about fourteen mortal hours.

The Brigade was asked to do too much, and when at last they staggered out of action, the men jumped and started at the rustle of a twig. It's a miserable thing when brave men are asked to do more than brave men can do.

One thing that added to the panic was that none, at least among the men and junior officers, knew anything at all about the trench. They thought they were going to storm the hill. So that things were so contrived that the bewilderment of a surprise should be added to the terrors of the volley. You will scarcely believe this perhaps. I have just come from having tea with the Argyle and Sutherland. Of the eight or ten officers there, not one had heard of the trench.

Here, by the river, I have talked to a score of Highlanders, and not one had heard of it either. They "didn't know what the hell was up" when the volley came. We could scarcely have provided all the elements of a panic more carefully.

Nothing of note followed during the day. Airlie fended off a Boer flanking move on our right, and the Coldstreams backed up the Highlanders a bit, but practically only the Highland Brigade was in it. It was a disaster to that Brigade only, and consequently the rest of the army does not feel itself defeated, and is not in any way discouraged. Some people suggest now that we in our turn may be attacked, and that the enemy may try and retake the river position from which we shifted him a fortnight ago. It is reported that they have got up heavy reinforcements from Natal, and some long-range guns that will reach our camp from the hill. All kinds of rumours are afloat, mostly to the effect that the Boers are circling round behind us, via Douglas on the west and Jacobsdal on the east, and mean cutting our communications. However, as I have long since found out, a camp is a hot-bed of lies. Nothing positive is known, for every one is kept in careful ignorance of everything that is going on. The idea is that the British soldier can only do himself justice when the chance of taking anything like an intelligent interest in his work is altogether denied him. The consequence is he is driven to supply the deficiency out of his own imagination. Ladysmith has already been taken and relieved at least a dozen times, and Mafeking almost as often. To-day Buller is on his way to Pretoria; tomorrow the Boer army will be marching on Cape Town.

As for our own little army, we have been digging ourselves in here, and are perfectly secure, and I daresay we shall be able to keep open the line all right. As to relieving Kimberley, that is another thing. Cronjé evidently doesn't think we can, for he has just sent us in a message offering us twenty-four hours to clear out in. He is a bit of a wag is old Cronjé.

RECONNAISSANCE

Bivouac on the Modder, January 15, 1900

RECONNAISSANCE
Bivouac on the Modder, January 15, 1900

At Modder River camp the dust lies thick and heavy. Every breeze that blows lifts clouds of it, that hang in the air like a dense London fog, and mark the site of the camp miles and miles away. The river, more muddy than ever, moves languidly in its deep channel. There is a Boer *laager* some miles above the camp, the scourings of which—horrid thought!—are constantly brought down to us. The soldiers eye the infected current askance and call it Boervril. Its effect is seen in the sickness that is steadily increasing.

Thank goodness we escape it. An advantage of scouting is, that, when it comes to a standing camp, with its attendant evils of dirt, smells, and sickness, your business carries you away, in front, or out along the flanks, where you play at hide-and-seek with the enemy, trap and are trapped, chase and are chased, and where you bivouac healthily and pleasantly, if not in such full security, at some old Dutch farm, where probably fowls are to be bought, or milk and butter; or under groups of mimosa trees among stoney deserted *kopjes*, where there is plenty of wood for burning, as likely as not within reach of some old garden with figs in it ripening and grapes already ripe.

One of the little pictures I shall remember belonging to Modder camp is the sight of the soldiers at early mass. You can picture to yourself a wide, flat dusty plain held in the bent arm of the river, with not a tree or bush on it; flat as a table, ankle-deep in grey dust, and with a glaring, blazing sun looking down on it. The dust is so hot and deep that it reminds one more of the ashes on the top of Vesuvius—you remember that night climb of ours?—than of anything else.

Laid out in very formal and precise squares are the camps of the various brigades, the sharp-pointed tents ranged in exact order and looking from far off like symmetrical little flower-beds pricked out on the sombre plain.

A stone's throw from the river is a mud wall, with a mud house at one side scarcely rising above it, yet house and wall giving in the early morning a patch of black shadow in the midst of the glare. Here the old priest used to celebrate his mass. A hundred or two of Tommies and a few officers would congregate here soon after sunrise, and stand bareheaded till the beams looked over the wall, when helmet after helmet would go on; or kneel together in the dust while the priest lifted the host. Every man had his arms, the short bayonet bobbing on the hip; every brown and grimy hand grasped a rifle; and as the figures sink low at the ringing of the bell, a bristle of barrels stands above the bowed heads. Distant horse hoofs drum the plain as an orderly gallops from one part of the camp to another. Right facing us stands Magersfontein, its ugly nose with the big gun at the end of it thrust out towards us. How many of this little brotherhood under the mud wall, idly I wonder, will ever see English meadows again?

The Boers still face us at Magersfontein. Their left is south of the Modder. They have a strong laager at Jacobsdal on the Reit, and have pushed west and south of that, where, from the kopjes about Zoutspan and Ramdam, they threaten our lines of communication. The Reit river, flowing almost south and north for some distance parallel to the railway, though a good way east of it, is a strengthening feature for them in that part of the field, and taking advantage of it, they have brought their left well round.

Their right, on the other hand, is scarcely brought round at all, but stretches about east and west, following the course of the Modder, and extending as far west as Douglas, fifty miles from Modder camp. They make raids south. Pilcher the other day cut some of them up at Sunnyside and took Douglas, but evacuated it again, and it is now in their hands. Altogether you can compare the Boer attitude to a huge man confronting you, Magersfontein being his head, his left arm brought round in front of him almost at right angles to his body and his right stretched wide out in line with his shoulders. From time to time he makes little efforts to bring these outstretched arms farther round, as if to clasp and enfold the British position at Modder River, and it is with the special object of observing and reporting on these movements that our scouting is carried on. This is now attended to by fifteen of us only, under Chester Master, the rest of the corps, with the Major, having gone down to join French at Colesberg now that the advance here has ceased. On the east side of the line we patrol the plain nearly to Jacobsdal, and often lie in the grass or sit among the rocks and watch the little figures of Boers cantering along the road that leads south by the river. Further scouting in that direction is carried on by the garrison along the line.

A strong reconnaissance of ours the other day (January 9th) in the direction of Jacobsdal was a very dignified and solemn exhibition. Our guns rumbled forward with their eight-horse teams across the plain, while our cavalry, stretched out in open order at fifty yards apart, traversed the country in long strings that might have been seen and admired by the enemy at a distance, I daresay, of twenty miles. Chester Master took us forward on the left close to the river, where a party of the enemy, stealing up from the river-bed, tried to cut us off—there were only six or eight of us—and chivied us back to the main body as hard as we could go, two miles *ventre à terre* through the pelting rain, blazing away from horseback all the time at us, but naturally doing no harm. We thought we should lead them into a trap when we lifted the rise, but our troops had all halted far back in the plain, and our pursuers turned as soon as they saw them. However, we got some men to join us, and set to work to chase them as they had done us. It was really quite exciting; little bent figures of horsemen with flapping hats on ahead, bundling along for dear life, each with its spot of dust attending, we following, whooping and spurring. But bustled as they were, the Boers knew the way they were going. There are some narrow belts of bush that run out from the river into the plain, and as we neared one of these, *crick-crack, crick-crack*, the familiar croaking voices of Mausers warned us against a nearer approach. We dismounted and fired away vaguely at the distant foe, not so much with the idea of hitting anything, but it is always a relief to one's feelings. I don't know why the guns didn't come up, but was told that they didn't like to push on too far, as the Boers were supposed to be in force here. It seemed a pity to miss such a good shot, especially as we had an enormous great escort and an open country back to camp. But that is the way with guns; sometimes they rush up to within 500 yards of the enemy before they shoot, and sometimes they won't shoot at all.

The afternoon was spent in carrying out our reconnaissance. A reconnaissance is undertaken with a view to exposing the enemy's position and strength. Without intending a real attack, you demonstrate, feign a forward movement, push on in one place or another, or threaten to turn his flanks; so obliging him to move his men here and there, expose his strength and the limits of the position, and, perhaps, the whereabouts and number of his guns, if they should be tempted to open fire at our scouts. This is the theory of the thing. In practice it doesn't quite work, owing to the utter ignorance of the Boers of all military tactics. On all occasions when we have carried out these manoeuvres, notably round the Magersfontein hills before the battle, they have not only failed to make the proper responses to our moves, but have neglected to take notice of them in any way whatever. Not a gun speaks, not a man is to be seen. We demonstrate before empty hills. Creepily, you may conjecture the fierce eyes along the rock edge, but nothing shows. In vain we circle about the plain, advance, retire, curtsey, and set to him; our enemy, like the tortoise, "will not join the dance." Nothing is more discouraging. It is like playing to an empty house. However, as young B—— said to me, we did our part anyway, and if they are so ignorant as not to know the counter-moves, well, they must take the consequences. Manoeuvres of this kind, I must tell you, are a high test of military skill, and are often not fully intelligible to the lay mind. As an instance of this, I heard a man of ours, a shrewd fellow but no soldier, say, in his coarse Colonial way, as we were riding home, that he "was glad we had finished making a b——y exhibition of ourselves." It is to be hoped that after a little we shall get to appreciate these manoeuvres better. Just at first there is a slight suggestion of Gilbert and Sullivan about them.

SCOUTING ON THE MODDER
Thornhill Farm, January 30, 1900

SCOUTING ON THE MODDER
Thornhill Farm, January 30, 1900

On the eastern or Jacobsdal side the country is all a plain, dull and monotonous like a huge prairie, with no shade from the heat or shelter from the thunderstorms. On the western side it is very different. Great hills run roughly parallel to the river course, but leave a wide plain between themselves and it. They are clothed with a few scant bushes, out of which their tops rise bare and rocky; but in the shady hollows and gorges the low thorn-trees (mimosas) grow thickly, and over the plain that stretches to the river their grey foliage gathers into thick covers or is sometimes dotted here and there. The smell of the mimosa flowers (little yellow balls of pollen-covered blossom) is the most delicious I know, and the air as we ride through these lonely covers, where a few buck seem the only tenants, is fragrant with it. Far apart there are farms, prettily situated, generally close to the hills, the rocky sides of the kopjes rising behind, the wide plain spread in front. Each has its dam, sometimes more than one, built round with mud embankments, with huge weeping willows overhanging, and rows of tall poplars and blue gums (with shreds of bark rattling), and plenty of other trees. The farmhouses themselves are uninteresting, but the gardens, with their great thicket hedges of prickly pear and quince and brilliant blossoming pomegranate, are delightful, especially at this time, when the fruit is just getting ripe.

It was out on this western side, where we were feeling for the enemy's right flank, some twenty miles from camp, in a niche half way up the mountain, that we spent our last Christmas. We rather expected an attack, as a Kaffir of ours had been taken by them, and might be expected to reveal our movements. After dark we climbed the hill, dragging our ponies over the boulders and scratching our way through the thorns.

The Boer hill was four or five miles distant, north across the plain. All along its purple sides we ranged with our glasses, seeing nothing; but after dark several little points of light showed where their laager was. We sat all night among the rocks (I thought of you and the roast-turkey and holly), occasional heavy drops of rain falling, and a flicker of lightning now and then. Heavy clouds rolled up, and the night set in as dark as pitch. The level plain below us lay flat as a pancake from their hill to ours. So passed our '99 Christmas, picturesque possibly, but not very comfortable. Dark hillside; rain in large warm drops; night dark, with a star or two and struggling moon. In front, a distant hillside, with points of camp-fire twinkling, where the Boers, indifferent to our little party, were carousing and drinking their dop. Now and then a yawn or groan as a man stretches his cramped limbs. Down below under us an expanse of dark plain, like a murky sea, reaching to our feet, which we peer across, but can make out nothing. Peep-of-day time is the Boer's favourite hour for a call, and we were all very much on the qui vive when the white line showed along the east. No doubt, however, they all had such heads after their Christmas drink that they were in no humour for such a diversion. At any rate, they let us alone. Very stiff and weary and wet, we crept down the hill soon after daybreak and started on our twenty-mile homeward march. It was 5 P.M. before we reached camp, and we had had nothing to eat all day. I don't know if we were most tired or hungry. Take that three days as a sample of work. We start at 6 A.M. on Sunday; do a full day's riding and scouting, and get three hours' sleep that night at Enslin. Then we saddle up and pass the rest of the night and all the next day riding, except when we are climbing hills on foot to look out. The second night we sit among the hills expecting an attack, and next day till one o'clock are in the saddle again. *À la guerre comme à la guerre.* Three days and two nights' hard work on three hours' sleep. And all this time you are drinking champagne (well, most of it, anyway), and sleeping in soft beds with delicious white sheets, and smoking Egyptian cigarettes, and wearing clean clothes, with nice stiff collars and shirt cuffs, and having a bath in the morning, warm, with sweet-smelling soap (Oh, my God!), and sitting side by side at table, first a man and then a woman; the same old arrangement, I suppose, knives to the right and forks to the left as usual. Ho! ho! There are times I could laugh. No doubt we shall all get redigested as soon as we get back, but meantime, as a set-off to the hardship, one knows what it is to feel free. We eat what we can pick up, and we lie down to sleep on the bare ground. We wash seldom, and our clothes wear to pieces on our bodies. We find we can do without many things, and though we sometimes miss them, there comes a keen sense of pleasure from being entire master of oneself and all one's possessions. Your water-bottle hangs on your shoulder; your haversack, with your blanket, is strapped to your saddle; rifle, bandolier, and a pair of good glasses are your only other possessions. As you stand at your pony's side ready to mount, you may be starting for the day or you may be away a fortnight, but your preparations are the same.

Above all others does this scouting life develop your faculties, sharpen your senses of hearing and of seeing, and, in practical ways, of thinking too; of noting signs and little portents and drawing conclusions from them; of observing things. You feel more alive than you ever felt before. Every day you are more or less dependent on your own faculties. Not only for food and drink for yourself and your pony, but for your life itself. And your faculties respond to the call. Your glance, as it scans the rocks and the plain, is more wary and more vigilant; your ears, as you lie in the scrub, prick themselves at a sound like a Red Indian's, and the least movement among cattle or game or Kaffirs, or the least sign that occurs within range of your glasses, is noticed and questioned in an instant.

This you get in return for all you give up—in return for the sweet-smelling soap and the footman who calls you in the morning. Oh, that pale-faced footman! It is dawn when, relieved on look-out, I clamber down the rocks to our bivouac. A few small fires burn, and my pal points to a tin coffee cup and baked biscuit by one of them. It is the hour at home for the pale-faced footman. I see him now, entering the room noiselessly with cautious tread as if it were a sick-room, softly drawing a curtain to let a little light into the darkened apartment, and approaching with a cup of tea that the poor invalid has barely to reach out his hand to. Round our little camp I look, noting trifles with a keen enjoyment. Shall I ever submit to that varlet again? No, never! I will leap from my bed and wrestle with him on the floor. I will anoint him with my shaving soap and duck him in the bath he meant for me. Do you know the emancipated feeling yourself? Do you know the sensation when your glance is like a sword-thrust and your health like a devil's; when just to touch things with your fingers gives a thrill, and to look at and see common objects, sticks and trees, is like drinking wine? Don't you? Oh, be called by twenty footmen and be hanged to you!

This Christmas patrol of ours was of use in touching the southernmost and westernmost limits of the Boer position. It has shown that the enveloping movement of which so much has been said, and which has been pressed now and then on the east side, has not made much progress on the west.

The big mountain range, running east and west, comes to an end some thirty miles west of Modder Camp, where it breaks up into a few detached masses and peaks. The extreme one of these, a sugar-loaf cone, is called the Pintberg, and on this lonely eerie a picket of ours is generally placed; crouched among the few crags and long grass tufts that form its point, the horses tethered in the hollow behind; listening by night and watching by day. When we come out thus far, we sometimes stay out a week or more at a time. The enemy's position is along the hills north of the plain by the river—chiefly north of it, but in places south.

I am turning over my diary with the idea of giving you a notion of the sort of life we lead, but find nothing remarkable.

"Last night, Vice, Dunkley, and I were on lookout on the *kopje*. There had been a heavy storm in the afternoon and another broke as we reached the hill. We crouched in our cloaks waiting for it to pass before climbing up, as the ironstone boulders are supposed to attract the lightning (I have heard it strike them; it makes a crack like a pistol-shot, and Colonials don't like staying on the hill tops during a storm). We passed all night on our airy perch among the rocks, half wet and the wind blowing strong. It was a darkish and cloudy night, rather cold. Watched the light die out of the stormy sky; the lightning flickering away to leeward; wet gleams from the plain where the water shone here and there; moaning and sighing of wind through rock and branch. We were relieved by Lancers in the morning and jogged back to Thornhill, where our little camp is, and I am writing this in the shade of a big mimosa close to the garden wall.

"I have seen prints in shop windows of farms and soldiers, bits of country life and war mixed, a party of Lancers or Uhlans calling at some old homestead, watering their horses or bivouacking in the garden. Often what I see now makes me think of these subjects. A large camp is hideous and depressing; dirty and worn, the ground trampled deep in dust; filth and refuse lying about; the entrails and skins of animals, flies, beastly smells, and no excitement or animation. But these outlying scenes, scouts, pickets, &c., have a peculiar interest. This garden, for instance, is itself pretty and wild, with its tangle of figs, its avenue of quinces (great golden fruit hanging), its aloes all down the side, with heavy, blue spikes and dead stems sticking thirty feet in air, branching and blackened like fire-scorched fir-trees, and its dark green oranges and other fruit and flower-trees all mixed in a kind of wilderness; and behind this the steep kopjes, with black boulders heaped to the sky, and soft grey mimosas in between. It is a pretty spot in itself, but what a different, strange interest is brought in by the two or three carbines leaning against the wall, the ponies, ready saddled, tethered at the corner, the hint of camp-fire smoke climbing up through a clump of trees, and now and then a khaki-clad figure or two passing between the trunks or lying under them asleep."

Here is another little extract, a bit of a night-spy by three of us on the west side, where we had heard that the Douglas commando was establishing a laager near a drift some thirteen miles below camp; a move forward of their right arm, if true.

"The night was dark as pitch, and very windy, just what we wanted. After missing our way several times, whispering, consulting, and feeling about in the dark, we came on the wattle fence and beehive huts of a Kaffir kraal. Up to this we crept, and Vice dived into the hole of an entrance, and after some underground rumblings emerged with an old nigger as you draw a badger from his earth. The old man was soon persuaded by a moderate bribe to be our guide to the spot we wished to reconnoitre. He told us that parties of Boers were pretty often round that way, and that one had passed the previous night at the kraal. Dunkley agreed to stay with the horses, and Vice and I went on with the Kaffir. The country was grassy, with plentiful belts and clumps of silvery bush. After a while the moon shone out and the clouds dispersed, which made us feel disagreeably conspicuous in the white patches between the bush."

Exmoor, as far as the contour of the ground is concerned, is a little like the more up-and-down parts of the veldt, and scouting there would be very much like scouting here. For instance, suppose your camp was at Minehead, the Boers being in strength at Winsford, and a report comes in that they have pushed on a strong picket to Simonsbath. This rumour it is your business to test. With two friends on a dark, windy night you set out. You leave the road and take to the moor. You ride slowly, listening, watching intently, keeping off the high ground, and as much as possible avoiding sky-lines. At some cottage or moorland farm you leave the horses and creep forward on foot, working along the hollows and studying every outline. If they are at Simonsbath, they will have a lookout on the hill this side. A British picket would show its helmets at a mile, but the Boers don't affect sky-lines. They will be on this side, with the hill for a background, and very likely right down on the flat; for though by day the higher you are the better for seeing, yet at night, when your only chance is to see people against the sky, the lower you are the better. These points and others you discuss in whispers, crouched in the dark hollows, and then creep forward again.

"Vice and I crawled to the top of our ridge at last just as morning was breaking. There were bushes and rocks to hide among, and the clouds had all gone, and day broke clear. The deep river ravine lay right below us, and as the light penetrated, the first thing we saw was a small shelter tent with a cart or waggon by the side of it. We grinned and nudged each other and wagged our heads at the discovery, but kept them carefully hidden. Farther west was a detached *kopje*, the site of a permanent Boer picket, according to the Kaffir; but there was no regular laager. There were no horses grazing about, no cattle, no smoke, none of the usual and inevitable signs. A picket! Yes. Pushed out from Koodoosberg, the big hill which rises abruptly from the plain three or four miles off, but no real occupation. After studying the country yard by yard with our glasses, and making a few notes about the lie of the land and the names and positions of farms, we creep off and get back to camp by mid-day."

The results of these exciting little prowls, when worth while, are sent in to the General, and from the mass of evidence thus placed before him he is supposed to be able to define the enemy's position and movements.

Chester Master and our little body were paid a pretty compliment by the General the other day; for the Major having written to ask if we might join him, Methuen replied that he was sorry to have to refuse, but that we were doing invaluable work, and he really couldn't spare us.

Well, fare you well. We hear of heavy reinforcements arriving. They will be very welcome. Magersfontein, Colenso, Stormberg; we could do with a change. But what a revelation, is it not? Are these the prisoners that we played at dice for? One thing in it all pleases me, and that is the temper and attitude of England. I like the gravity, the quiet, dogged rolling up of the shirt-sleeves much better than the blustering, wipe-something-off-a-slate style which the papers made so familiar to us at the beginning.

THE ADVANCE
Modder River Camp, February 13, 1900

THE ADVANCE
Modder River Camp, February 13, 1900

We are back in the old camp, but only for a few hours. This afternoon we march. Yesterday, crossing the line, we had a glimpse of Rimington and the rest of the corps. They have come up with French, and are off eastward on the flank march. We shall be after them hotfoot before dark. Things begin to shape themselves. We are going to bring our right arm round, leaving Magersfontein untouched, and relieve Kimberley by a flank march in force. Methuen stays here. Poor fellow! I wish him joy of it. Bobs and Kitchener direct the advance; French heads it. They say we shall march 50,000 strong. The line is choked with troop trains, batteries, siege guns, naval guns, and endless truckloads of stores and provisions. At last! is every one's feelings. The long waited for moment has come. You know a hawk's hover? Body steady, wings beating, and then the rushing swoop. So with the army. We have hovered steady here these two months with our wings stretched. Now we swoop.

Far out on the left flank our little body of fifteen has been in a great state of suspense for several weeks. We knew the great tide of advance was setting up from Orange River to the Modder, and as no orders came for us, we began to think we should be out of it. Then one evening, as I was sitting on some boulders above camp looking out over the country, I saw Chester Master riding in from headquarters with a smile on his face, and the sort of look that a man has who brings good news. Down I clambered. Yes, it had come. We were to move that night. The advance had begun, and we were off on an all-night march to catch up French. What a change came over the men! Instead of bored, sulky faces, and growlings and grumblings, all were now keen and alert. When the moon rose we started. Our very ponies seemed to know they were "in the movement," and stepped out cheerily. The night was clear as silver, and each man's shadow moved by his side, clean cut on the ground like the shadows thrown by the electric light outside the Criterion. Song and joke passed once more, and soon up went the favourite cavalry march, the most stirring tune of any, "Coming thro' the Rye." It was very jolly. Not often has one ridden on such a quest, on such a night, to such a tune as that.

So, old Modder, fare you well! Farewell the huge plain that one grew so fond of, with its blue and yellow bars of light, morning and evening; the shaggy *kopjes* heaped with black rocks, the secluded, lonely farms nestling beneath, old Cook's, where the figs were ripe in the garden, and Mrs. Dugmore, who gave us fresh bread and butter and stewed peaches. Not soon shall I forget those morning patrols. The sea of veldt, the pure air, the carelessness, the comradeship, and the freedom. Old Gordon has a good verse that I find sometimes running in my head—

It was merry in the morning
Among the gleaming grass,
To wander as we've wandered many a mile,
And blow the cool tobacco cloud
And watch the white wreaths pass,
Sitting loosely in the saddle all the while.

And then the secret bivouacs and lurking-places along the river or in among the deserted hills. The lookout from the tall pyramid, where I have kept watch so many hours day and night, in heat of sun or with stars glittering overhead.

It was from this *kopje* that we got notice to quit, by the way. Our notice taking the shape of several little brown-backed Boers galloping about and spying at us from a hill one and a half miles to the north. That night we drew out in the plain after dark and camped (no fires) among the bushes, and at grey dawn stole back to have another look. Back dashes one of our advance scouts to tell us that a big force of Boers was just rounding the point. Next minute we were swinging out into the plain, through the low scrub and thorn bush, and as we did so the Boers came through the Nek. They must have known exactly where our usual camp was, and crept up overnight to cut us off. It wasn't by much that they missed. Three or four loiterers, as it was, had a warm minute or two. The first single shots grew to a sudden fierce crackle, like the crackle of a dry thorn branch on the fire, as they came through the bush. But they came on nevertheless, one horse hit only, and joined us, and we formed up and started at a steady gallop for the hills beyond the plain, six miles off; where there was a quite strong camp, established a few days before, for which we have lately been scouting. The Boers chased us some way, but we had got a long start, as they came through the rough ground, and they were never on terms with us. Still it was near enough. Five minutes earlier and what a slating we should have got!

We were told afterwards that the plan on this side was to draw the Boers south of the hills, so as to give the cavalry, which was to move westward just north of the range, a chance of cutting them off. The cavalry, however, didn't turn up. No one seemed to know what had become of them, and I daresay they were saying the same of us. The advice not to let your left hand know what your right hand is doing is sometimes rather too literally followed in these manoeuvres, I think. Meantime the Boers have driven off all old Cook's cattle and all Mrs. Dugmore's too; and as we were sent out with the express object of "reassuring the farmers," the result is not entirely satisfactory.

No matter; this was all a side issue; now for a larger stage and more important operations. Blow trumpets and sound drums. Enter Lord Roberts and the main army.

Relief of Kimberley
Kimberley Club, February 18

RELIEF OF KIMBERLEY
Kimberley Club, February 18

It is with feelings of the deepest satisfaction that I look at the address at the head of this notepaper. Indeed for the last five minutes I have been staring at it dreamily without putting pen to paper, repeating "Kimberley Club, Kimberley," to myself, vaguely thinking of all it portends; the varied fortunes of the last three months; the cheery setting out; the first battles, that already seem so long ago; the repulse, and long, dreary wait by Modder; the gradual reconstruction of the whole plan of attack, and now the final achievement. Christian and I have been sharing a pint of champagne in the club bar. It was not till I heard the bottle pop that I realised, as by a sudden inspiration, that the British army had really attained its object at last. Very gravely we gave each other luck, and gravely drank our wine. Both of us, I am glad to be able to tell you, rose to the occasion, and as we looked across the bubbles, no foolish chaff or laughter marred the moment.

I wrote you my last letter from old Modder just as we were leaving to catch French. Marching light and fast, we got up with him on the night of the 15th at the Klip Drift on the Modder, northeast of Jacobsdal. From there we were sent back to guide on Kitchener, which we did, bringing him to French's camp on the river by 6 A.M. next morning (16th). We met on the way our little ambulance cart bobbing home with the adjutant languidly reclining. He had had one of those escapes that now and then come off.

There was a high hill to the north, and up this the previous morning, R., an active walker, had climbed to have a view of the country. He reached the top, which is like a gable, slanting both sides to a thin edge, and precisely as he did so, ten or a dozen great hairy Boers reached it from the other side, and, at ten yards' distance across the rock edge, their eyes met. Can you conceive a more disgusting termination to a morning stroll? Without a word said, R. took to his heels and the Boers to their Mausers. Down the hill went R., bounding like a buck, and all round him whipped and whined the bullets among the rocks. Twice he went headlong, twisting his ankle badly once as the stones turned underfoot; but he reached the bottom untouched and the shelter of the bluff where he had left his pony, jumped on and dashed out into the plain and under the Boer fire again, and got clean away without a scratch, him and his pony. Was ever such luck?

French started on his final relief march about an hour later, and we were not able to accompany him as our horses were absolutely done up. It was very disappointing at the time to see him ride off on this last stage with a large party of our comrades, led by Rimington himself (he was first into Kimberley, we heard afterwards) at the head. However, as things turned out, it did not much matter, for the next day we had an interesting time, and saw a big job put in train, which is not finished yet, and which we shall probably see more of if we start, as they say, tomorrow.

The thing began at grey dawn. Chester Master and two or three Guides were sent forward to reconnoitre a *kopje* where the Boers the day before had had a gun. We found the gun gone. Some marks of blood, a half-dug grave, and two dead horses, showed that the fire of our long naval gun had been more or less effective. We then rode on, the column we were guiding getting gradually into formation, and we were just mounting the next ridge, when down in the valley beneath we saw a long line of waggons, stretching away eastward for miles, dragged by huge bullock teams. They were making the best of their way forward, each with a party of mounted men riding at the side, and at the first glance, so close to our army and camp were they, I almost fancied it must be a convoy of our own. However, we realised what was up pretty quickly. The Boers, hearing of French's flank march, and fearing they would be cut off if they remained, were abandoning their position in the hills about Magersfontein, which they had intrenched so strongly, and were quietly and promptly moving off towards Bloemfontein. The rearguard of their line was at that moment just opposite to us.

Chester Master immediately sent back an orderly as hard as he could go to tell our fellows what was in front and hurry them up, every moment being now of the utmost importance if we wanted to intercept the enemy. The Boers themselves took their measures instantly and with their usual coolness. A long line of *kopjes* ran eastward across the plain, flanking the line of their march, and directly they saw they were discovered, their horsemen dashed forward and began to occupy these, thus guarding the right flank of their retreat from our attack. Seeing this, Chester Master galloped back himself to urge on our Mounted Infantry, who were now mustering rapidly to the attack.

From the *kopje* on the extreme left front, where we were, we could now see extended at our feet the whole plan of the approaching battle, while as yet the two sides were invisible to each other. In the valley on the north side of the *kopjes* the Boers were urging on their convoy and rapidly despatching their sharpshooters to hold the hills along their right. On the south side were the masses of our columns, with the squadrons of Mounted Infantry now detaching themselves from the main body, and beginning to stream across the level plain towards the same hills; all with heads bent one way, horses prancing and pulling, and with all the signs of eager excitement, as though they divined, though as yet they could not see, the presence of the enemy. Over the dusty plain they canter, but they are too late by a few minutes. The Boers are there already, and as the Mounted Infantry come along, passing close beneath us, an outbreak of rifle-fire occurs, and the dry plain, which is of perfectly bare earth, is dotted with little white puffs of dust as the bullets strike along it. The fire is a bit short, but schooled by this time in "kopje tactics," and realising what is coming, our squadrons very prudently pull up and wait for the guns. They haven't long to wait. I always love to see the guns come up. Over stones and rocks and bushes, six strong horses at the gallop, the drivers lashing the off horses, the guns jumping and rumbling and swinging; then the yell, "Action front," and round come the teams with a splendid sweep; next instant they are cast off and jingle to the rear, and the little venomous guns are left crouching like toads, looking towards the enemy; the gunners are upon them before they are at a standstill (everything happens simultaneously); there is an instant's pause while the barrel rises, and then comes the naked spurt of fire, no smoke, and the officer steps clear of the dust and glues his glasses to his eyes as the shell screams on its way. Within ten minutes of our first viewing the enemy, half a battery had got into action near our *kopje*, and was bombarding the first hill along the enemy's flank.

Two or three of the Boer waggons, the last of the line, had been abandoned when their retreat was first discovered. These we took possession of, and with them two Dutchmen and some coloured boys, one of whom had been driver to a field-cornet of Cronjé's. From him we learnt that Cronjé had definitely abandoned the whole Magersfontein position, that this was the tail of his force going through, and that consequently there was nothing to be feared from a rear attack. Chester Master wrote a hasty despatch to this effect to Kitchener and gave it to me, after which I had a most amusing ride through our lines from the extreme left to the extreme right, where Kitchener was. First by our batteries, thundering and smoking (the enemy only had one gun in action that I saw, but I must say it did very well, feeling for the range with two short shots, and after that getting well into our guns every time), and then on through the Mounted Infantry, who kept on charging and retiring, until finally after three miles' ride I came to the far right, where Kitchener and the big naval gun sat together in state on the top of a small *kopje* strewn with black shining rocks.

Here I gave in my despatch, "From Captain Chester Master, left front, sir," and the best military salute I have yet mastered (inclined to go into fits of laughter at the absurdity of the whole thing all the time), and the great man, with his sullen eye, sitting among his black rocks all alone, reads it and asks me a question or two, and vouchsafes to tell me that the information is "very important," which I suppose meant that he had not been certain whether he was in contact with the middle or extreme tail of the enemy's force. Various officers of the staff come up and I tell them all I know. I am very hungry and parched with thirst, but I know I shall get nothing out of these fellows. However, my luck holds. Under some thorn-trees below I spy the flat hats of the sailors, and under the lee of an ammunition waggon hard by a group of officers. All is well. Five minutes later I am pledging them in a whisky and sparklet, and sitting down to such a breakfast as I have not tasted for weeks. God bless all sailors, say I!

Orders meantime come thick and fast from the grim watcher on the rocks above, and troop after troop of Mounted Infantry go scouring away to the attack. It is a running fight. *Kopje* after *kopje*, as the Boers push on, breaks into fire and is left extinct behind. But still they keep their flank unbroken and their convoy intact. For the hundredth time I admire their dogged courage under these, the most trying of all circumstances, the protection of a slow retreat.

So it goes on through the day, and I have great fun galloping about on my own account, looking into things here and there, and watching the general progress of events. I meet Chester Master again about 5 P.M., and he asks me to ride forthwith to Kimberley with him if Flops can stand it. All the Boer force has cleared from Magersfontein (our information was all right) and is in retreat on Bloemfontein, and Kitchener is sending word by Chester Master to French, bidding him right turn and march to head off the Boer retreat, while he (Kitchener) hangs on their tail.

An hour later we start; four of us. Chester Master, myself, May, and a black boy. It is a twenty-three mile ride. A full moon is in the sky but clouds obscure it, which is a good thing, as the country is being traversed by stragglers of theirs, leaving the hills and in retreat eastward. We hear of several such fugitive bodies from our pickets for the first few miles. Then we are in absolute solitude. The plain lies bare and blanched around us. A thorn bush or two sticks up on it, or, now and then, the ghastly shape of a dead horse lying in puffed up relief with legs sticking out stiff and straight and an awful stench blowing from it. Kimberley's search-light at stated intervals still swings its spoke over our head.

Six or seven miles out from Kimberley my pony gives out, and Chester Master and May on fresh horses ride on, leaving me the boy. We plod on, an interesting, delicious ride. I get off and walk. A little wind rustles over the dry earth and bushes, but otherwise there is not a whisper of sound. The landscape at one moment lies white before us as if it had been washed in milk, and the next is blotted out with clouds. Now and again we pause to listen, and the boy stands like a bronze image of Attention with bent head and held breath, the whites only of his eyes moving as he rolls them from one object to another. At last from a low *kopje* top by the path comes the first loud and welcome "Halt! Who goes there?" of an English picket. Another two or three miles brings me to an outpost of the town, and there, dead tired and Flops the same, I fling myself on the ground, after hearty greetings and a word or two of talk with the guard, and do a three hours' sleep till the dawn of the 17th.

In a grey light I rouse myself to look out across the wet misty flat, hearing some one say, "Who's that? What force is that?" followed immediately by "Call out the guard; stand to your arms, men." But then, as light increases, we see by the regular files and intervals that the force is British, and I know that Chester Master has got in all right and delivered his message, and French already, at a few hours' notice, is casting back with that terrible cavalry of his after Cronjé and the retreating Boers.

Kimberley does not in the least give one the idea of a beleaguered and relieved town. There are a few marks of shells, but so few and far between as not to attract attention, and you might walk all about the town without being struck by anything out of the common. I have sampled the roast-horse and roast-mule which the garrison seems to have been chiefly living on for the past five or six weeks, and find both pretty good, quite equal, if not superior, to the old trek-ox. Some people tell us pathetic stories of the hardships to women and young children and babies, owing to the difficulty of getting proper food, especially milk. On the other hand, many seem to have actually enjoyed the siege, and two or three young ladies have assured me that they found it infinitely diverting and enjoyed an excellent time, making up afternoon tea-parties among their friends. The relief was not the occasion of any excitement or rejoicing whatever. People walked about the streets and went about their business and served in their shops without showing in their appearance or manner any trace of having passed through a bad time or having been just delivered from it. They seemed, on the whole, glad to see us, but there was no enthusiasm. This was partly due, I think, to the absence of drink. The Colonial's idea of gratitude and good-fellowship is always expressed in drink, and cannot be separated from it, or even exist without it. Many felt this. Several said to me, "We are awfully glad to see you, old chap, but the fact is there's no whisky." On the whole, except the last week, during which the Boers had a hundred-pounder gun turned on, one doesn't gather that the siege of Kimberley was noteworthy, as sieges go, either for the fighting done or the hardships endured. But that is not to reflect on the defenders, who showed a most plucky spirit all through, and would have resisted a much severer strain if it had been brought to bear upon them.

PAARDEBERG—THE BOMBARDMENT
February 24, 1900

PAARDEBERG—THE BOMBARDMENT
February 24, 1900

We are once more upon the Modder. I should think
the amount of blood, Dutch and English, this river has
drunk in the last few months will give it a bad name for
ever. There is something deadly about that word Modder.
Say it over to yourself. Pah! It leaves a taste of blood in
the mouth.

We have been fighting in a desultory kind of way for
the last week here. Coming from Kimberley, where we
had gone to holloa back French (you could follow him
by scent all the way from the dead horses), we made a
forced march and rejoined him here by the river, where
he is busily engaged, with Kitchener at the other end, in
bombarding old Cronjé in the middle. They have fairly
got the old man. Kitchener had stuck to him pretty tight,
it seems, after we left them that evening at Klip Drift.
French has nicked in ahead. Macdonald has arrived, I believe, or is arriving, and there are various other brigades
and divisions casting up from different quarters, all concentrating on unhappy Cronjé. Lord Roberts, I suppose,
will get the credit, but part of it, one would think, belongs
to Kitchener, who planned the movement and put it in
train before Lord Roberts arrived.

Cronjé, by all accounts, has about 4000 men with him.
He has dug himself into the river banks, which are steep
and afford good cover. You would never guess, sweeping
the scene with your glasses, that an army could be hid-

ing there. The river curves and winds, its course marked by the tops of the willows that grow along its banks. The land on both sides stretches bare and almost level, but there are a few rises and knolls from which our artillery smashes down its fire on the Boer laager. At one point you can make out a ragged congregation of waggons, broken and shattered, some of them burning or smouldering. That is where the laager is, but not a soul can one see move. The place looks an utter solitude, bare and lifeless in the glare of the sun. There is no reply to our busy guns. The little shrapnel clouds, stabbed with fire, burst now here now there, sometimes three or four together, over the spot, and the blue haze floats away, mingling with the darker, thicker vapour from the less frequent lyddite. "What are they shooting at?" a stranger would say; "there is nobody there." Isn't there? Only 4000 crafty, vigilant Boers, crowding in their holes and cuddling their Mausers. Ask the Highlanders.

You will have heard all about that by this time. The desperate attempt last Sunday to take the position by storm. It was another of those fiendish "frontal attacks." Have we been through Belmont and Graspan and Modder River and Magersfontein for nothing? Or must we teach every general in turn who comes to take charge of us what the army has learnt long ago, that a frontal attack against Mausers is leading up to your enemy's strong suit. For Methuen there were reasons. Methuen could not outflank, could not go round, was not strong enough to leave his lines of communication, and had practically no cavalry. He had to go straight on. Belmont, Graspan, and Modder were turnpike gates. The toll was heavy, but there was no choice but to pay. But what was the reason of this latest? We had them here safely bottled up. We have them still. It is only a question of days. The attack could have gained nothing by success; has lost little by its failure. The casualties were 1500. I know all about eggs and omelettes, but these were simply thrown in the gutter.

Never tell me these Boers aren't brave. What manner of life, think you, is in yonder ditch? Our artillery rains down its cross fire of shells perpetually. The great ox-waggons are almost totally destroyed or burnt. The ammunition in the carts keeps blowing up as the fire reaches it. The beasts, horses and oxen, are strewn about, dead and putrid, and deserters say that the stench from their rotting carcasses is unbearable. Night and day they have to be prepared for infantry attacks, and yet, to the amazement of all of us, they still hold out.

Old Cronjé's apparent object is to try and save Bloemfontein by delaying us till reinforcements come up from the south and east. This is really what we want, because the more of the enemy we get in front of this great army of ours, the harder we shall be able to hit them. But evidently Cronjé is ignorant of our strength.

Meantime we can make out in our break-of-day scoutings up the river that bodies of men are approaching from the east. They have made a laager about ten miles up, and evidently mean to dispute our passage to the capital. The longer old Cronjé holds out, the more men from Colesberg and Natal will come up, the more entrenchments will be cut, and the harder will be our way to Bloemfontein. 'Tis the only way he sees to save the town, for we should march straight in else. Perhaps, too, he cherishes some hope of being relieved himself; of a determined attack from without, which might enable him, by a sudden sally, to break through; though, for dismounted men (and their horses are all dead by this time), the chances of ultimate escape in a country like this must be very small, one would think. Anyhow, he sticks to his work like a glutton. The shells burst over them. The lyddite blows them up in smoke and dust, the sun grills, the dead bodies reek, our infantry creep on them day and night; foul food, putrid water, death above and around, they grin and bear it day after day to gain the precious hours. And all the time we on our side know perfectly well that no relief they could possibly bring up would serve our army for rations for a day.

PAARDEBERG—THE SURRENDER
March 5, 1900

PAARDEBERG—THE SURRENDER
March 5, 1900

Well, that is over, and I hope you are satisfied. We have got Cronjé. His victories are o'er. We have also got Mrs. Cronjé, which was a bit more than we bargained for. They cut her an extra deep hole, I hear, to be out of shell-fire, and she sat at the bottom all day long, receiving occasional visits from Cronjé, and having her meals handed down to her. One can fancy her blinking up at her "Man," whom she always, I am told, accompanies on his campaigns, and shaking her head sorrowfully over the situation. There is nothing very spirit-stirring about a mud hole and an old woman sitting at the bottom of it, but the danger and the terrible hardships were real enough. That is always the way with these Dutch. They have all the harsh realities and none of the glamour and romance. Athens, with their history and record, would have made the whole world ring for ever. But they are dumb. It seems such a waste.

Albrecht too is among the prisoners, the famous German "expert," who designs their works for them and manages their artillery; and we have taken 4000 prisoners, and several guns and one detested "pompon." Come, now, here is a little bit of all right at last.

I was one of a party that rode down with the Major on the morning of the surrender to the *laager* and saw the prisoners marched in. They seemed quite cheery and pleased with themselves. They were dressed in all sorts of ragged, motley-looking clothes; trousers of cheap tweed, such as you see hung up in an East End slop-shop; jackets once black, now rusted, torn and stained, and battered hats. They reminded me more of a mob of Kent hop-pickers than anything else, and it was a matter of some surprise, not to say disgust, to some of us to think that such a sorry crowd should be able to withstand disciplined troops in the way they did.

I talked to several of them. They all agreed in saying that they had been through the most ghastly time in the last ten days and were heartily glad it was over. They exchanged nods and good-days with us and the soldiers who were standing about, and altogether seemed in a very friendly and conciliatory mood. All this, however, it struck me, was rather put on, a bit of acting which was now and then a trifle overdone. Boers are past-masters at hiding their real feelings and affecting any that they think will be acceptable. It is a trait which has become a national characteristic, and the craft, dissimulation, *the slimness*, as it is called, of the Boers is a by-word. I suppose it comes from the political situation, the close neighbourhood of a rival race, stronger and more energetic, which fosters in the stolid Dutchman, by way of buckler, this instinctive reticence and cunning. His one idea is to make what he can out of the situation without troubling his head for a moment about his own candour and sincerity. It is Oriental, the trait you expect to find in a John Chinaman, but which surprises you in a burly old Dutchman. Still there it is. At any farm you go to, men, women, and children will put on a semblance of friendship, and set to work to lie with a calmness which is really almost dignified. No one in this country ever believes a thing a bit the more because a Dutchman says it.

We went on into the captured *laager*. It was an extraordinary, interesting, and loathsome sight. Dead bodies of horses and men lay in all directions in various stages of decomposition, and the reeking smell was something quite indescrib able. I fancied, even after leaving the place, that I carried the smell about with me, and that it had got into my clothes. The steep river banks were honeycombed with little holes and tunnels, and deep, narrow pits, like graves; narrow at the top, and hollowed out below to allow less entrance for shells. Evidently each man had cut his own little den. Some were done carelessly, mere pits scooped out. Others were deep, with blankets or old shawls spread at the bottom, and poles with screens of branches laid across the top to keep off the sun. I saw one or two which were quite works of art; very narrow tunnels cut into the side of the river-cliff, and turning round after you entered, making a quite secure retreat, unless perhaps an extra heavy old lyditte might happen to burst the whole bank up. This actually happened, they told us, with the very last shot fired the night before; a bit of the bank having been blown up with eight men in it, of whom five were killed and three wounded. The whole river channel looks as if a big colony of otters or beavers had settled here, honeycombing the bank with their burrows, and padding the earth bare and hard with their feet. It was all worn like a highroad. On the other side, the waggons were a sight; shattered, and torn, and wrecked with shot; many of them burnt; several, huge as they are, flung upside down by the force of a shell bursting beneath them. All their contents were littered and strewn about in every direction; blankets, clothes, carpenters' and blacksmiths' tools, cooking utensils, furniture. You would have thought the Boers were settlers moving to a new country with all their effects, instead of an army on the march. This is how they do things, however, in the homely, ponderous fashion. They often take their women and children with them. There were many in the crowd we captured.

I wandered about alone a long time, looking at the dismal, curious scene where so much had been endured. White flags, tied to poles or stripped branches, fluttered from waggon tops. Our ambulance carts came along, and the Tommies, stripping to the waist, proceeded to carry, one by one, the Dutch wounded through the ford on stretchers.

We are bivouacked ourselves far up the river, in a secluded nook among mimosas and *kopjes* with the thick current of the lately unknown, but now too celebrated, Modder rolling in front of us. The weather has changed of late. It is now autumn. We have occasional heavy rains, and you wake up at night sometimes to find yourself adrift in a pool of water. It gets chilly too.

The enemy are all about the place, and we interview them every morning at daybreak, sometimes exchanging shots, sometimes not. We lay little traps for each other, and vary our manoeuvres with intent to deceive. This advance guard business (we are dealing here with the relief parties of Boers that have come up between us and Bloemfontein) always reminds me of two boxers sparring for an opening. A feint, a tap, a leap back, both sides desperately on the alert and wary.

We lost poor Christian yesterday in one of these little encounters. He was mortally wounded in stopping at short range to pick up a friend whose horse had been shot. I have mentioned him, I think, to you in my letters. There was no one in the corps more popular. "Tell the old dad I died game," was what he said when the Major, coming up with supports, knelt down to speak to him.

Nothing very noteworthy has occurred since the surrender. The army has been quietly resting, taking stock of the prisoners, and sending them to the railway, and we are expecting every day now the order to advance. The enemy, meanwhile, have been collecting in some force, and are evidently prepared to dispute our march east. Yesterday we had a duel with a gun which they have managed, goodness knows how, to drag up to the top of a commanding hill some miles up the river. However, it was too strongly placed. We lost several men. The enemy's fire was very accurate, and they ended up by sending three shots deliberately one after the other right into our ambulance waggons.

We shall be able to post letters today, and the reason this one is so extremely dirty is that I am finishing it in a drizzling rain, being on picket guard a couple of miles up the river, not far from the scene of yesterday's shooting. The Boers are on the bustle this morning. One can see them cantering about on the plain just across the river, where thousands of their cattle are grazing. In front the big-gun hill glimmers blue in the mist. Two or three of the enemy have crept up the woody river-course and tried a shot at us; some close; the bullets making a low, quick whistle as they flit overhead. My two companions—there are three of us— are still blazing an indignant reply at the distant bushes. By the amount of fire *tap, tap,* tapping like an old woodpecker all round the horizon, it seems that there is a sudden wish for a closer acquaintanceship among the pickets generally this morning. Those fellows in the river are at it again!

Poplar Grove
March 8, 1900

Poplar Grove
March 8, 1900

We left our camp on Modder River at midnight of the 6th. The night was clear and starlit, but without moon. Moving down the river to take up our position in the flank march, we passed battalion after battalion of infantry moving steadily up to carry the position in front. The plan is this. The infantry advance up the river as if to deliver a frontal attack; but meanwhile the mounted troops, which have started during the night, are to make a wide detour to the right and get round at the back of the Boer position, so as to hem them in. The idea sounds a very good one, but our plans were upset by the Boers not waiting to be hemmed in. However, it is certain that if they had waited we should have hemmed them in. You must remember that.

The guns go rumbling past in the darkness. We are on the right of the column. Along our left we can just distinguish a long, black river of figures moving solidly on. It flows without break or gap. Now and then a jar or clank, the snort of a horse, the rattle of chains, rises above the murmur, but underneath all sounds the deep-toned rumbling of the wheels as the English guns go by.

Close in front of us is a squadron of Lancers, their long lances, slender, and black, looking like a fringe of reeds against the fast paling sky, and behind us there is cavalry without end. The morning is beautifully clear with a lovely sunrise, and that early hour, with horses fresh, prancing along with a great force of mounted men, always seems to me one of the best parts of the whole show.

As soon as we can see distinctly we make out that we have got to the south of the enemy's hills, and are marching along their flanks. They look like a group of solid indigo pyramids against the sunrise. Are those *kopjes* out of range? is a question that suggests itself as we draw alongside, leaving them wide on our port beam. Yes, no! No! a lock of smoke, white as snow, lies suddenly on the dark hillside, followed by fifteen seconds of dead silence. Then comes the hollow boom of the report, and immediately afterwards the first whimper, passing rapidly into an angry roar of the approaching shell, which bursts close alongside the Lancers. "D—d good shot," grunts the next man to me, with sleepy approval, as indeed it is.

The order to extend is given, but before the Lancers can carry it out the smoke curl shows again, and this time the shell comes with a yell of triumph slosh into the thickest group of them, and explodes on the ground. There is a flutter of lances for an instant round the spot, and the head and mane of a shot horse seen through the smoke as it rears up, but the column moves steadily on, taking no notice, only now it inclines a little to the right to get away from that long-range gun.

We march on eastward as day broadens, through a country open and grassy, rising and falling in long slopes to the horizon. Suddenly from the far side of one of these ridges comes the rapid, dull, double-knocking of the Mausers. The enemy are firing at our flankers; these draw back under cover of the slope, and we continue to advance, the firing going on all the time, but passing over our heads. Now the Major, curious as to the enemy's position, sends half-a-dozen of our troop up the slope to get a view. These ride up in open order, and are at once made a mark of by the Boer riflemen, luckily at long range. *Wing, wing,* with their sharp whirring note, came the bullets. They take a rapid survey and return to tell the Major that the scenery in that direction is exceptionally uninteresting, a long slant of grass stretching up for a mile or more, and somewhere about the sky-line Boers shooting. Then comes the usual interval while we wait for "the guns." The guns shortly arrive and a brace of Maxims. These open a hot fire at the top of the hill. They are rather in front of us, and fire back up the slope across our front; the bullets passing sound like the rushing of wind through grass.

After a bit the order is given to take the hill, and we advance firing as we go. Beyond the guns and Maxims other men are moving up. You notice that the Colonials shoot as sportsmen do. The regulars blaze away all the time, seeing nothing, but shooting on *spec* at the hill top; load and shoot, load and shoot, as hard as they can. Our fellows have a liking for something to shoot at. With their carbines at the ready, they walk quickly forward as if they were walking up to partridges. Now a man sees a head lifted or the grass wave, and instantly up goes the carbine with a crack as it strikes the shoulder. Another jumps up on to an anthill to get a better view. Every time an extra well directed shell falls among the prostrate Boers, one or two start up and run back, and noticing this, several of the Guides wait on the guns, and as each shell screams overhead on its way to the hill top, they stand ready for a snapshot. *Wang!* goes the shell, up leaps a panic-stricken Dutchman, and *crack, crack, crack*, go half-a-dozen carbines. Though absolutely without cover, the enemy keep up for some time a stubborn reply, and when at last we reach the crest, tenanted now only by a few dead bodies, we have lost nearly two precious hours. Below across the vast plain the Dutch are in full retreat. It is doubtful already if we shall be able to intercept them.

The doubt is soon decided against us. We are crossing the flat, kopjes in front and a slope on the right. Suddenly several guns open from the kopjes ahead, the shells dropping well among us. At this coarse behaviour we pause disgusted. An A.D.C. galops up. We are to make a reconnaissance (hateful word!) on the right to see if the slope is occupied. "Will the Guides kindly ...?" and the officer waves his hand airily towards the hill and bows. We are quite well aware that the slope is occupied, for we have seen Boers take up their position there, and several experimental shots have already been fired by them. However, "anything to oblige" is the only possible answer, and the squadron right wheels and breaks into a canter. Once on the rise the bullets come whizzing through our ranks quick enough. Down goes one man, then another, then another. Maydon of *The Times*, who is with us, drops, but only stunned by a grazing bullet, as it turns out. The Life Guards deploying on our left catch it hot, and many saddles are emptied.

A charge at this time would have scattered the Boers instantly (they were very weak) and saved both time and lives. Instead of this, however, it is thought more advisable to keep every one standing still in order to afford a more satisfactory test of Boer marksmanship. It is very irksome. The air seems full of the little shrill-voiced messengers. Our ponies wince and shiver; they know perfectly well what the sound means. At last the fact that the hills are held is revealed to the sagacity of our commanders, and we are moved aside and the guns once more come into action.

It is easy (thank goodness!) to be wise after the event. I find every one very discontented over this action, and especially the cavalry part of it. Had we made a good wide cast instead of a timid little half-cock movement, and come round sharp, we should have intercepted the Boer convoy. As it is, we lose two more hours at this last stand which brings us till late in the afternoon, and soon afterwards, on approaching the river, we see five miles off the whole Dutch column deliberately marching away eastward. Our failure stares us in the face, and we see with disgust that we have been bluffed and fooled and held in check all day by some sixty or eighty riflemen, while the main body, waggons, guns, and all, are marching away across our front. "The day's proceedings," says one of our officers to me with laughable deliberation, "afford a very exact representation of the worst possible way of carrying out the design in hand."

BLOEMFONTEIN

Bloemfontein

My last letter was written after Poplar Grove, and we marched in here six days later on the 13th. Of the fighting on the way I can give you no account, as I was knocked up with a bad chill and had to go with the ambulance. Unluckily we had two nights of pouring rain, and as I had left behind my blanket and had only my Boer mackintosh (with the red lining), I fared very badly and got drenched both nights and very cold. This brought on something which the doctor described as "not real dysentery." However, whatever it was (or wasn't), it made me as weak as a baby, and I was transferred to our ambulance, in which I lay, comfortable enough, but only vaguely conscious of my surroundings.

The next day, the 10th, they fought the battle of Spytfontein. All I remember of it was some shells of the Boers falling into the long river of convoy which stretched in front of me in an endless line, and the huge bullock and mule waggons wheeling left and right and coming back across the veldt, with long bamboo whips swaying and niggers uttering diabolical screams and yells. We lost a good many men, but did fairly well in the end, as our infantry got into the enemy among some hills, where there were not supposed to be any enemy at all, and cut them up a good deal.

The following day I made the march on a bullock-waggon, which is really a very fine and imposing way of getting along. Your team of twenty strong oxen, in a long two-by-two file, have a most grand appearance, their great backs straining and the chain between taut as a bar, and the view you get over the field from your lofty perch among the piled-up kits and sacks is most commanding. There used to be an old print at home of Darius at the head of the Persian host "o'erlooking all the war" from the summit of some stately chariot or other, which much reminded me of my present position. I managed to mount my pony to ride into Bloemfontein, which we did on the 13th, and am now quite well.

This morning I sent you a wire to tell you that I had got my commission, thinking thereby to impress you with the importance of the event. The past five months of trooper life have not passed unpleasantly. There have been the inconveniences and hardships of the moment, *les petites misères de la vie militaire*, which sound trifling enough, but are rather a tax on one's endurance sometimes. The life of a trooper, and especially of a scout, is often a sort of struggle for existence in small ways. You have to care for and tend your pony, supplement his meagre ration by a few mealies or a bundle of forage, bought or begged from some farm and carried miles into camp; watch his going out and coming in from grazing; clean him when you can, and have an eye always to his interests. Your life and work depend so entirely on your pony that this soon becomes an instinct with you. Then there are your own wants to be supplied. You will be half starved often if you can't raise something to put in your pocket—eggs from a Kaffir, or a fowl, or a loaf of bread. Then there is the cooking question. Wood is scarce; unless you or your pal have an eye to this, you may go supperless for want of a fire. Another scarcity is water. Very likely there will be none nearer than a mile from camp, and this means a weary tramp after a long day. Then what about your bedding? You can carry only a blanket or greatcoat on your horse, so that, when you are away from your convoy, which is often enough, you have not much covering, and if it comes on to rain you have a poor time of it. Of clothes, too, you have only what you ride in. If wet, they dry on you; and few and far between are your chances of washing them. All these things sound and are trifles. A man would think little of them in a sporting expedition in the Himalayas; but after a long time the monotony tells. The heat tells. You are sometimes "a bit slack," and at those times the cooking of your wretched morsel of flesh, or the struggle for a drop of pea-soup coloured water becomes irksome.

The little star on your shoulder saves you from all that. You can tell the new commissioned man by the way he has of constantly looking over his shoulder. Poor fellow! he likes to catch the pretty glitter—the *twinkle, twinkle, little star*—that lifts privates' hands to him as they pass. Some one else cooks for him now, and there is the officers' mess cart with a few welcome extras and a merry gathering at meals and a batman to tend the pony (though you keep an eye on that yourself too), and extra clothes and blankets, and a shelter of some sort to sleep under, and a Kaffir boy to put out his washing things when he comes in hot and tired, and altogether life seems, by comparison, a very luxurious and pleasant affair. I am a bit of a democrat, as you know, and all for equality and the rights of man; but now I say, like Mesty, when they made him a butler, "Dam equality now I major-domo."

Bloemfontein is a pretty little place, but it takes you by surprise. The country round is, for endless leagues, so barren, a mere grassy, undulating expanse of prairie land, with a few farms at ten-mile intervals, that the appearance of a town seems incongruous. All of a sudden you come to a crowd of low bungalow-like roofs under the shadow of some flat-topped *kopjes* and realise the presence in this void of the Free State capital.

The place is suggestive, in its low single storey houses and pretty gardens, of quiet ease, and has a certain kindliness about it. It is pleasant to see the creeper grown fronts and flower patches, and few shady trees after our long sojourn in the veldt. But the one memorable sight of the place, the scene of a special and unique interest, is the Bloemfontein Club. This is the first time that the great army under Lord Roberts has found itself in occupation of any town, and the first time, therefore, that all its various contingents have had a chance of meeting together in one place. At the Bloemfontein Club the chance has occurred, and certainly never before, in any time or place, could you have seen such representative gatherings of the British race from all parts of the world as you will see if you stroll any day into the verandah and smoking-room and bar of the Bloemfontein Club. From the old country and from every British colony all over the world these men of one race, in a common crisis, here for one moment meet, look into each others' faces, drink, and greet and pass on; to be drawn back each to his own quarter of the globe and separated when the crisis is passed and not to meet again. But what a moment and what a meeting it is, and what a distinction for this little place. Organise your mass meetings and pack your town-halls, you never will get together such a sample of the British Empire as you will see any afternoon in this remote pothouse. What would you give for a peep at the show; to see the types and hear the talk? You would give a hundred pounds, I daresay. I wish I could take you one of these afternoons: I would do it for half the money.

You can see the great mountain of Thaba Nchu quite clearly from here, though it is forty miles away, and trace every ravine and valley in its steep sides, defined in pure blue shadows. We have been out there these last ten days on what is known as a "bill-sticking" expedition; distributing, that is, a long proclamation which Lord Roberts has just issued, in which he explains to the Free State Burghers that all their property will be respected, and they will be allowed themselves to return to their farms forthwith if they will just take a little quiet oath of allegiance to the British Crown. A few have done so and received passes, but the interest taken in the scheme seems less on the whole than one would have supposed likely. Some explain it by saying that the Boers are such liars themselves that they can't believe but what the English are lying too; while others think the move is premature, and that the Free State is not prepared yet to abandon the war or her allies.

We were by way also of endeavouring to cut off any stray parties of Boers who might be making their way north from Colesberg and that neighbourhood. Broadwood was in command of us. There was a stray party, sure enough, but it was 7000 strong. It passed across our bows, fifteen miles east of us, and we let it severely alone.

Meantime there is a general lull. In the midst of war we are in peace. I am going off tomorrow to our old original Modder River camp (having ridden in from Thaba Nchu yesterday), that cockpit where so much fighting was done and where we spent so many weary weeks watching the heights of Magersfontein, to get luggage and things left behind. It will be strange to see the old place deserted and to ride near the hills without being shot at. Buller is peacefully sleeping at or near Ladysmith; the sound of his snoring faintly reaches us along the wires. Gatacre slumbers at Colesberg. Kitchener has disappeared, no one knows exactly where; and Little Bobs has curled himself up at Government House here, and given orders that he is not to be called for a fortnight. What news can you expect in such times? There is positively none.

Bloemfontein gives one the curious impression just now of a town that has been unpacked and emptied of all its contents, and had them dumped down on the land alongside. The shops contain little or nothing. They have been bought up and have not had time to restock. But outside the town, on the veldt, a huge depot of all sorts of goods is growing larger and larger every day, as the trains, one after another, come steaming north with their loads of supplies. There is a street, ankle deep in mud, of huge marquees, each with a notice of its contents outside: *Accoutrements, Harness, Clothing, Transit Store,* and what not. Behind and between are vast piles of boxes, bales, bags, and casks heaped up, and more arrive every hour on loaded trucks along a branch rail from the station. It is a busy, animated scene. Orderlies run or gallop about; quartermasters and adjutants and others hurry here and there, with their hands full of papers from one marquee to another, collecting their orders; shopping as it were, but shopping on rather a large scale; and the big ox-waggons come creaking along and churning up the mud. This is where the cost of a war comes in. These are a few of the little things that our army will require on its way to Pretoria. There will be money to pay for this. We shall feel this some day, you and I.

And poor unstuffed Bloemfontein lies there empty. There are all the shops, and here all the merchandise. You may guess that the tradesmen are indignant. Never has there been such a market. Here is the whole British army clamouring for all kinds of things; most furiously perhaps for eatables and drinkables, *baccy* and boots. All these things have long been bought up, and the poor Tommies can only wander, sullen and unsated, up and down the streets and stare hungrily in at the empty shop windows; while out of the empty shop windows the shopkeeper glares still more hungrily at them. I have heard how in the Fraser River the fish positively pack and jostle as they move up. So here; but the unhappy sportsman has nothing to catch them with. Brass coal-scuttles and duplex lamps are about all that remains in the way of bait, and these are the only things they won't rise to. He rushes off to Kitchener. "Give me a train a day. Give me a train a week." "You be d—d," growls Kitchener. Back he comes. The hungry eyes are still staring. Incarnate custom flows past. Never in all his life will such a chance recur. Poor wretch! It is like some horrible nightmare.

MODDER REVISITED
Bloemfontein, April 9, 1900

MODDER REVISITED
Bloemfontein, April 9, 1900

All the way from Modder River down the Kimberley line and up the central one from Naauwpoort, the most dismal rumours reached me at all stations, growing more definite as I neared Bloemfontein. Sanna's Post and Reddersberg! You have heard all about them by now. Nearly 1000 casualties and seven guns taken.

You remember I told you in my last letter that a big body of Boers marched north across our bows. Pilcher was out on that side and drew back. The Boers got wind of him, and wheeled west in pursuit. Broadwood, not strong enough to hold Thaba Nchu, moved in on Bloemfontein, the Boers after him.

It is no fun describing things one has not seen. The ground I know. It is a flat plain the whole way, but down the middle of it is a deep sluit or watercourse, some thirty feet deep, with steep, sudden banks, and through this the road dips down and passes. Broadwood halted on the east side of it, thus leaving it between himself and home. In doing this he gave a chance to an enemy who never throws a chance away. The Boer leader was Christian De Wet.

The first thing in the morning the enemy began shelling our camp. The convoy was sent on, not a scout with it. Meantime, during the night several hundred Boer marksmen had been sent round into the sluit, and were now lying right across poor Broadwood's retreat. The Boers, acting with their devilish coolness as usual, took possession of the waggons without giving the alarm. Our two batteries and Roberts' Horse came along, and were allowed to get to point-blank distance, and then the volley came; magazine rifles at pistol-shot range. For the moment the result, as at Magersfontein, was chaos.

Hornby dealt the first counter-blow. With the five manageable guns he galloped back a bit and brought them into action at 1000 yards. He showed first that it was going to be a fight and not a stampede. "Steady and hit back," said Q Battery. You should hear the men talk of that battery. It lost almost every man, killed or wounded, but it was the chief means in restoring some sort of order to the retreat. But the disaster was past retrieving. In killed, wounded, and prisoners we lost a third of our force, the whole convoy, and seven guns out of twelve. I can see the question you are dying to ask. Why on earth did Broadwood camp the wrong side of that ditch? That is exactly the sort of question that a "blooming civilian" would ask. And then came Reddersberg and the loss of another five hundred. Christian De Wet again! And all this within hearing, as you may say, of the main British army.

These disasters come most inopportunely for us. Many of the Orange Free State Burghers, when their capital was taken, seem to have thought it was all up and some of them took the oath. But this right and left of De Wet's has changed that impression. It comes just in time to fan into a fresh blaze embers that seemed dying out. We hear that all the farmers who had taken the oath are under arms again. They had not much choice, for the fighting Boers simply came along and took them.

My visit to old Modder River was very interesting. It was quite deserted; only a few odds and ends of militia, where, when I remember it last, there were stately great squares of ordered tents and long lines of guns and limbers and picketed horses, and the whole place crawled with khaki, and one felt around one all the bustle and energy of a huge camp. I felt quite melancholy, as when one revisits some scene of childhood changed beyond recall. Trains were running regularly up to Kimberley and ordinary citizens were travelling up and down. It seemed the war was forgotten. To me, who had been living in the head and front of a big army for seven months, all these old signs of peace and a quiet life seemed strange enough. There were some children going up with their papas and mamas. As we came one after another to the lines of hills at Belmont and Graspan they pointed and crowded to the windows, and papa began to explain that the great fights had been here, and to tell all about them, quite wrong.

The hills look peaceful enough now. The children press their noses and little india-rubber fingers against the glass, and chatter and laugh and bob up and down—

Little they think of those strong limbs
That moulder deep below.

And I sit back in my corner ashamed of my dirty old tunic and the holes in it, and peer between two small flaxen heads at hills I last saw alive with bursting shell.

At Modder village I hired a horse and rode across the plain to Magersfontein. I must often have described the place to you—the great flat and the beak of hill, like a battleship's ram, thrust southward into it. Do you know, I felt quite awestruck as I approached it. It seemed quite impossible that I, alone on my pony, could be going to ride up to and take single-handed that redoubtable hill, which had flung back the Highlanders, and remained impregnable to all our shelling. I thought some Boer, or ghost of a Boer, would pop up with his Mauser to defend the familiar position once more. However, none did. I picked my way through the trench, littered with scraps of clothing and sacks and blankets, with tins and cooking things, and broken bottles and all sorts of rags and debris littered about. The descriptions of the place sent home after the battle are necessarily very inaccurate. Those I have seen all introduce several lines of trenches and an elaborate system of barbed wire entanglements. There is only one trench, however, and no barbed wire, except one fence along a road. There are, however, a great number of plain wire strands, about ten yards long perhaps, made fast between bushes and trees, and left dangling, say, a foot from the ground. They were not laid in line, but dotted about in every direction, and, in anything like a dim light, would infallibly trip an advancing enemy up in all directions. The single trench is about five feet deep, the back of it undercut so as to allow the defenders to sleep in good shelter, and the number of old blankets and shawls lying here showed it had been used for this. It followed closely the contour of the hill, about twenty yards from its base. Eastward it was continued across the flat to the river.

The "disappearing guns," in the same way, were not disappearing at all. They simply had strong redoubts of sandbags built round them, the opening in front being partly concealed by bushes. On each side of the gun, inside the redoubt, was a pit, with a little side passage or tunnel, where two or three gunners could lie in perfect security, and yet be ready at an instant's notice to serve their gun. As for the kopjes themselves, every rock and stone there was split with shell and starred with bullet marks. The reverse side of the slopes were steepened with stone walls here and there, as a protection against shrapnel, and sangars and lookout places were built at points of vantage. Altogether, though not so elaborate as one had been led to believe, the defences struck one as extremely practical and business-like.

I stayed there for two interesting hours. You can guess with what feelings I looked down on the plain from Long Tom's redoubt, poor old Joey's rival, and traced the long line of the river, with its fringe of willows, and marked, up and down, a score of places where we had skirmished or hidden, distinguishing the positions of our guns and pickets, and all the movements and manoeuvres of our army. For the first time one realised what a bird's-eye view the Boers had of it all, and how our whole position and camp lay unrolled like a map almost at their very feet.

I must add a word to tell you that the boxes have arrived! I only wish you could have been here to see the contents distributed. First (this was about a week ago) came a huge box full of good things to eat, raisins, figs, a great many tins of cocoa and milk, chocolate, and other things. We spread them all out on sheets in the verandah of the farm in little heaps, and very pretty and tempting they looked, the white sheets down the shady verandah, and little piles of sweetmeats and things dotted all over them. Each man drew a ticket and chose his eatable, some putting it carefully away, others bolting it immediately. One can get absolutely nothing in Bloemfontein, and the men were as keen as school children. It was an excellent idea sending such a lot of figs and raisins. They are soon gone, but they are so immensely appreciated while they last; they give the men the badly wanted holiday feeling. I almost think that, in the way of provisions, delicacies are more liked by men on service, and really do them more good than the more practically useful things.

Then, a day or two ago, came another great box full of clothing. Flannel shirts, socks, under-clothing, &c. There was, especially, in this box, a packet of little handkerchiefs with a card, and on it written: "Worked by Mrs. Hope and her little girls for the soldiers." The little present touched us all very much. I have kept the card with the intention of thanking "the little girls" if ever I get the chance.

We are only about a hundred strong now, and there were enough things to go round several times. If you had foreseen and planned the date of their arrival they could not have reached us at a more opportune moment. The men have scarcely anything to wear, for all our kit and clothes, everything we possess, was lost at the Sanna Post surprise party. I assure you they are grateful. I read them the names of the subscribers, and they all send their best thanks. Several came up to me and asked that their thanks might be sent to you for your trouble in getting the subscriptions, &c. No money that could have been expended in any charity could have been better spent than this. The men have done fearfully hard work, and were many of them literally in rags. It has been the greatest help. The Major has sent you a few words of thanks, but has asked me to write more particularly. You will let those know who have helped, will you not, how this Colonial corps of ours has appreciated your English present.

And now, farewell. They say we move forward in a week. I hope it may be true. They also say we shall finish the campaign in a couple of months. Fiddle-de-dee! is what I say. Tell H. to educate little S. as a scout among the Devonshire hedges, and give him a bit of practical training against the time he will be old enough to come out. There will be Boers to take him on.

JUSTIFICATION OF THE WAR
Bloemfontein, April, 1900

JUSTIFICATION OF THE WAR
Bloemfontein, April, 1900

Yes, certainly, my own reason for fighting is plain and strong. I am fighting for a united South Africa. A united South Africa will, in my opinion, justify the war. The Boers are genuinely patriotic, I haven't a doubt. They have every right and reason to fight to the last for their freedom and independence. But the continued existence of independent States on the pattern of the Dutch republics in the midst of South Africa is bound to be a perpetual irritation. The development of the resources of the country will be checked. The effort to remain separate and apart has obliged, and will more and more oblige, these States to build themselves round with a whole system of laws specially directed to hamper immigration; and the richer are found to be the resources of the country, the more harassing and stringent will this system of laws have to become. In fact, in this great, free, and undivided country, to hedge a State round with artificial barriers of this sort, in order that it may enjoy a kind of obsolete, old-fashioned independence of its own, soon becomes intolerable. It is unjust to all the rest of the continent. The country, if it is to have its due weight and influence in the affairs of the world, must be united and make itself felt as a whole. It is not fair on such a country, young but rapidly developing, to take two of the richest tracts of it right in its midst and to say, "You may go ahead with the development of all the rest, but these two portions are to be left on one side, to drop out of the running, to be withered and useless members, and instead of contributing to the total, and joining in with the progress of the rest, are to do all in their power to impede the general advance."

It is bad enough when any naturally separate State shows the retrograde temper and an inability to profit by its own resources, but when that State is an integral part of one great and young continent, then its action becomes intolerable. I think it is not only the people in a country that have claims, but the country itself that has a claim. If you want South Africa to ripen ultimately into a great first-class world Power (and that is its claim), instead of a bunch of fifth-rate antagonistic States, the first thing to do is to range the country under one Government, and as a British Government will be progressive, and a Dutch one will certainly be retrograde, you must put it under a British one. That is the first essential, and if any genuinely patriotic instincts are overridden in the process, it is very sad, but it cannot be helped. Better this than that the whole country should miss its destiny.

As for the *Uitlanders* and their grievances, I would not ride a yard or fire a shot to right all the grievances that were ever invented. The mass of the Uitlanders (i.e., the miners and working-men of the Rand) had no grievances. I know what I am talking about, for I have lived and worked among them. I have seen English newspapers passed from one to another, and roars of laughter roused by *The Times* telegrams about these precious grievances. We used to read the London papers to find out what our grievances were; and very frequently they would be due to causes of which we had never even heard. I never met one miner or working-man who would have walked a mile to pick the vote up off the road, and I have known and talked with scores and hundreds. And no man who knows the Rand will deny the truth of what I tell you.

No; but the *Uitlanders* the world has heard of were not

these, but the Stock Exchange operators, manipulators of the money market, company floaters and gamblers generally, a large percentage of them Jews. They voiced Johannesburg, had the press in their hands, worked the wires, and controlled and arranged what sort of information should reach England. As for the grievances, they were a most useful invention, and have had a hand in the making of many fortunes. It was by these that a feeling of insecurity was introduced into the market which would otherwise have remained always steady; it was by these that the necessary and periodic slump was brought about. When the proper time came, "grievances," such as would arrest England's attention and catch the ear of the people, were deliberately invented; stories again were deliberately invented of the excitement, panic, and incipient revolution of Johannesburg, and by these means was introduced that feeling of insecurity I have spoken of, which was necessary to lower prices.

Not a finger would I raise for these fellows. And another war-cry which I profoundly disbelieve in, and which will probably turn out in the long run to be a hoax, is the "Dutch South Africa" cry. How any one who knows his South Africa, who knows the isolation of life among the farmers, and the utter stagnation of all ideas that exists among the people, can credit the Boers with vaulting ambitions of this sort, is always a surprise to me. I fancy such theories are mostly manufactured for the English market. Naturally I form my opinion more or less from the men in our corps who seem best worth attending to. They, most of them, have an intimate knowledge of the Colony and of one or both of the Republics, and I do not find that they take the "Great Dutch Conspiracy" at all seriously. Some people maintain that, though perhaps the Boer farmers themselves were not in it, yet their leaders were. But the farmers form the vast majority of the Boers. They are an independent and stiff-necked type; and it is as absurd to suppose that their leaders could pledge them to such vast and visionary schemes as it is to suppose that such schemes could have the slightest interest for them. As a matter of fact, what has given old Kruger his long ascendency is the way in which he shares and embodies the one or two simple, dogged ideas of the mass of the Burghers. "God bless the Boers and damn the British" are two of the chief of these, but they only apply them within their own borders.

But it's a case of the proof of the pudding. If this scheme for a general rising existed, why is not the Colony in arms now? What do you think the answer to that is? Why, that the plot did indeed exist and had been carefully matured, and that it would have come off all right if the Boers had marched boldly south; but that, for some unknown reason, their hearts failed them at the last moment, and they didn't dare go on and reap what they had sown. "If only they had marched on Cape Town, the whole Colony would have risen."

Doesn't it sometimes occur to you that, when his own interests are concerned, the Boer is a tolerably wide-awake gentleman, and that he knows how to look after those interests of his almost as well as we can teach him? Are you prepared to believe of him: first, that he laid down and organised this vast conspiracy; second, that he deliberately armed himself to the teeth with a view of carrying it out; third, that he chose his own time for war and declared it when he thought the moment was ripe; fourth, that he gained advantages to begin with, and had the Colony at his feet; and fifth, that he was seized with a sudden paralysis at the last moment, and found himself unable to march ahead and gather in the recruits who were on tip-toe to join him? No, no. If the plot existed, why didn't the plot work? It had every chance.

I will tell you what there was. There were a number of appeals and letters (some of them I have seen) from families in the north to their relations in the Colony, praying for sympathy, and perhaps for active help. But these were merely personal appeals. There is no hard and fast line, so far as the people are concerned, between the Colony, Orange Free State, and Transvaal. The same big families, or clans almost, have their branches in all three, and probably there is not a family of any consequence in either that has not a number of relations in the other two. Consequently as war drew closer the excitement and anxiety it caused spread southward from family to family. There was a good deal of sympathy felt, no doubt, by the Dutch in the Colony for their relations farther north, and there has been surreptitious help, information given, and sympathy. But there the matter has usually ended. There have been very few recruits, and there never was an organised conspiracy.

It is curious to notice how the several sections of the Dutch were picked up just as they were laid down. The most determined spirits of all, the most bitter against English rule, the irreconcilables, had fought their way farthest north, and formed the Transvaal. South of them came the Orange Free State, just across the Colony border—independent, but not so bitter; while in the Colony itself remained all those weaker brethren whose hearts had failed them in the Great Trek days, and who had remained under our government.

The present war has revealed these strata just as they were deposited. The northern State was the leader and aggressor. The southern one, drawn in by its fiercer neighbour, was still true to the cause. And so, too, the Dutch of the Colony were exactly today where they had been sixty years ago. They could no more join the war than they could join the trek. And, in spite of individual appeals to relations, &c., you may be sure that the northerners knew pretty accurately how the land lay. Their own action shows this.

Therefore, I put aside utterly, so far as I am concerned,

the *Uitlander* and Dutch conspiracy arguments, of which one hears so much, as things which, though they may occupy the attention of leading article writers in London, yet are not convincing, and have no smack of reality to any one who knows something about the *Uitlanders* from personal observation, and something about the Boers and Boer life from personal observation. I put these aside and come back to the only argument that will really wash, that has no clap-trap in it. And that is South Africa under one Government, and under a strong and progressive Government. Human nature is pretty much the same all the world over, and if the Boers have been to blame in the past, no doubt the Britons have been just as much to blame. Anyway, it is impossible and would be useless to strike a balance between them now. The fact that stands out salient and that has to be dealt with in the present is that South Africa is divided against itself; that it never can and never will step up into its proper place until it is united, and that, therefore, to fight for a united South Africa is to fight on the right side and in a good cause.

And one thing I much like this plain reason for is, that it makes it easy for one to do full justice to one's adversaries. I admire their courage and patriotism very much. I acknowledge fully their dogged obstinacy in defence and their dangerous coolness in retreat, and I am sorry for them, too, and think it a sad thing that such brave men should be identified with so impossible a cause. You must be careful how you believe the reports sent home by war correspondents. I suppose people like to hear harm of their enemies, and a daily paper's best business is to give the public what the public wants rather than what is strictly true. The consequence is that accounts of Boer fighting and of the Boers themselves (traitors and cowards are the commonest words) are now appearing which are neither more nor less than a disgrace to the papers which publish them. I don't know since when it has become a British fashion to slander a brave adversary, but I must say it seems to me a singularly disgusting one, the more so when it is coupled with a gross and indiscriminating praise of our own valour and performances.

THE MARCH NORTH
Near Johannesburg, May 31, 1900

THE MARCH NORTH
Near Johannesburg, May 31, 1900

"May 1st, 1900.—The long-looked, long-waited for moment has come at last. We march from Bloemfontein on a glorious autumn morning, in fresh cool air and the sky cloudless. Forty miles off Thaba Nchu, that hill of ill omen, might be ten, so bold and clear it stands up above the lower ranges. The level plain between the island hills is streaked with gauzy mist.

"North of Bloemfontein we get into a pretty, uneven country with several level-topped *kopjes* set end to end like dominoes, and thickets of grey mimosas clustering in the hollows. The great column is moving forward on our left. Big ambulance waggons, with huge white covers nodding one behind the other, high above the press; the naval twelve-pounders, with ten-oxen teams and sailors swinging merrily alongside; infantry marching with the indescribable regular undulation of masses of drilled men, reminding one of the ripple of a centipede's legs; field artillery, horse artillery, transport waggons, more infantry, more guns—they stretch in a long, dark river right across the plain.

"Now a halt is called. The men drop on one knee where they stand, or hitch up their knapsacks to ease their tired shoulders. Then on again, guns jolting, men sweating, marching at ease, with helmets on wrong side first to shelter their eyes, and rifles with butt-ends over shoulders. They have a rest after a few hours, and fall out by the wayside, fling off the heavy accoutrements, light pipes, and fall a-yarning, stretched on the grass, or pull out scraps of old newspapers to read."

That was written the day we left Bloemfontein, just a month ago, and 250 miles away. We have come along well, have we not?

Brandfort is a little town on the railway some forty miles north of Bloemfontein, overlooked by a big rocky kopje on the north. Here we find our dear friends once more assembled to meet us after this long interval, and we have a little battle with them, of which I will spare you the description. An incident of some interest was the appearance of the "Irish Brigade" from the Natal side, who held the hill above the town. Rimington got leave from Hutton to turn them out, which he did so cleverly, and taking us at them at such a pace that we did the business without loss, except, indeed, in horses, of which several were hit. I don't know if the two or three prisoners we took (and that we had some thought of shooting out of hand) were a fair sample of the brigade, but fouler-mouthed scoundrels I think I never set eyes on.

Our plan of advance has been all along very simple and effective. Our centre keeps the railway, while our wings, composed largely of mounted troops, are spread wide on each side, and threaten by an enclosing movement to envelop the enemy if he attempts to make a stand. These tactics have been perfectly successful, and the Boers have been forced again and again to abandon strong positions from a fear of being surrounded. A bear's hug gives the notion of the strategy. No sooner do our great arms come round than away slip the Boers while there is still time. The Vet River was probably their strongest position, and here they did make some attempt at a stand. This is how things looked that morning:—

"May 5th, 12.30.—We have just got to the big slopes overlooking Vet River. The enemy is in a strong position along the river-bed, which is thickly wooded, and in the hills beyond. Our left has touched them, and as I write this our pompon on that side has a couple of goes. Kaffirs tell us that the valley is full of Boers. Boers everywhere; in the river-bed, in the sluits on the far side, in the hills; and that they have plenty of guns. It is something like the Modder River position, but stronger, inasmuch as there are ranges of hills on the far side of and overlooking the river; so that they have two lines of defence, the second commanding the first. An excellent arrangement. Walking forward to the brow, a few of us had the whole panorama at our feet. We had no idea it was so strong, and you might notice a thoughtful look on more than one face as we walked back to our men behind the hill.

"We have now got the guns to a nearer rise, sloping to the river, and are standing in extended order waiting for the next move. This will take the form of artillery practice, and it is prophesied that we shall get it pretty hot, as they will certainly have better guns than our twelve-pounders. The sun is melting. Guns unlimber (1.15). Teams jingle back, and the guns open fire from edge of slope, each one as it delivers its shot starting back as if with surprise at its own performance.

"3 P.M.—Our guns are blazing away merrily

151

now. The Boers, if they have guns, are very reticent. They have sent us a few shells, which have done no harm, mostly falling short. Hamilton is said to be at or near Winburg. If this is so, he will be threatening the retreat of the Boers here soon. Meantime a huge column, miles long, is crawling in the distance across the flattish grass sweeps far to the east. This is the main column, under Lord Roberts."

We thought, you see, that we were in for quite a big fight. We thought the same often later. At this river or this range they will make their stand. But always, as here at Vet River, we advanced on such a wide front that the enemy had to retire betimes to avoid being outflanked, and so the "stand" was never made. We joined Ian Hamilton at Kronstad, and while we were out with him on the east side the enemy once or twice attacked our flank or rearguard in the most determined manner. However, we held on our way very composedly, our waggons rumbling along sleepily indifferent, while the Boers with all their might would be hanging on to our tail. Usually, after we had towed them for a day or two, they would let go, and then another lot would come along and lay hold. The first party would then retire to its own village and district, feeling, no doubt, that it had barked us off the premises in great style, and lay in wait for the next army of ten or twenty thousand men that should happen to pass that way.

It is the convoy that always hampers our movements so, that dictates the formation of an advance and makes us almost a passive target to attack. Our convoy with Ian Hamilton must have been seven or eight miles long, and was often delayed for hours at fords and creeks, where scenes of wild confusion took place and you were deafened with yelling Kaffirs and cracking whips. This convoy has of course to be guarded throughout, which means a very attenuated and consequently weakened force, an attack on one part of which might be carried on without the knowledge of the rest of the column, or the possibility of its giving much help anyway. When we left Lindley we had a sharp rearguard action, and the Boers pushed their attack very vigorously. They did the same on the right flank, and the advance guard also had some fighting. Neither of these parties knew that the others were engaged at all, and probably the bulk of the main column were quite ignorant that a shot had been fired anywhere.

Lindley is one of those peculiar, bare, little Dutch towns, the presence of which on the lonely hillside always seems so inexplicable. It is even more than usually hideous. There is the inevitable big church, the only large building in the place, occupying a central position, and looking very frigid and uninviting, like the doctrine it inculcates; a few large general stores, where you can buy anything from a plough to a pennyworth of sweets, and some single-storey, tin-roofed houses or cottages flung down in a loose group. But around it there are none of the usual signs of a town neighbourhood. No visible roads lead to it; no fertile and cultivated land surrounds it; no trees or parks or pleasure grounds are near it. The houses might have been pitched down yesterday for all the notice the *veldt* takes of them. Spread out over the hills and valleys for some hundreds of miles each side this barren treeless veldt, which, after all, is the main fact of South African life, seems to carry these little unexpected towns on its breast with the same ease and unconsciousness that the sea carries its fleets of ships; surrounding and lapping at their very hulls; not changed itself nor influenced by their presence.

During our stay of a day or two at Lindley it became increasingly evident that the people of that neighbourhood resented our presence there. Our pickets were constantly engaged. There are some rather abrupt hills on the east side of the town, among the nearer ones of which our look-outs were stationed while the Boers prowled among the others. Here the Mausers and Lee-Metfords talked incessantly, and the conversation was carried on in a desultory way down in the river valley and among the rolling hills on the southern side. It was plain that the enemy was quite prepared to "put up a show" for us, and no one was surprised, when the morning of our departure came, to see the strong force of Mounted Infantry told off for rearguard, or note the presence of the General himself in that part of the field.

There are long slanting hills that rise above the village on its south side, the crests of which were occupied by our pickets. As the pickets were withdrawn, the Boers rapidly followed them up, occupied the crest in turn, and began to put in a heavy fire and press hard on our retreating men.

From a square and flat-topped kopje just north of the town we had the whole scene of the withdrawal down the opposite slopes before our eyes. Our Mounted Infantry were hotly engaged but perfectly steady. They lay in the grass in open order, firing, their groups of horses clustered lower down the hill; then retired by troops and set to work again. This giving ground steadily and by degrees is a test of coolness and steadiness, and it was easy to see that our men were under perfect control. At last they came under the protection of our hill. We had got our battery of guns up it, and it was a moment of great satisfaction to all concerned, except possibly the Boers, when the first angry roar rose above the splutter of rifles, and the shell pitched among some of the foremost of the enemy's sharpshooters. In a duel of this sort the interference of artillery is usually regarded as decisive. Guns, as people say, have "a morale effect" that is sometimes out of proportion to the actual damage they inflict. Anyway, skirmishers seldom advance under gun-fire, and the Boers on this occasion were decisively checked by our battery. Even when the guns left, we were able from the vantage-ground of the hill to keep them at arm's length until the time came to catch up the column.

On the right flank they were more successful, pressing home a heavy attack on the Mounted Infantry on that side. A squadron got cut off and rushed by the enemy, who rode in to it shooting at pistol-shot distance, and shouting "Hands up!" We lost pretty heavily in casualties, besides about fifty prisoners. These small mishaps are of no great importance in themselves, but they encourage the enemy no doubt to go on fighting. The story as it goes round the farms will lose nothing in the telling. Probably in a very short time it will amount to the rout of Hamilton's column, and the captured troopers will lend a colour to the yarn. Burghers who have taken the oath of allegiance will be readier than ever to break it. However, time no doubt will balance the account all right in the long-run.

From Lindley, fighting a little every day, we marched north to Heilbron, where Broadwood got hold of the Boer convoy by the tail, and succeeded in capturing a dozen waggons. From there we cut into the railway, and crossed it at Vredefort, passing through the main body of the advance in doing so. Anything like the sight of these vast columns all pushing in one direction you never saw. In this country one can often see thirty or forty miles, and in that space on the parched, light-coloured ground you may see from some point of vantage five or six separate streams of advance slowly rolling northward, their thin black lines of convoy overhung by a heavy pall of dust. As we closed in and became involved for a moment in the whole mass of the general advance, though accustomed to think no small beer of ourselves as an army, for we number 11,000 men, we realised that we were quite a small fraction of the British force. Endless battalions of infantry, very dusty and grimy, but going light and strong (you soon get into the habit of looking attentively at infantry to see how they march); guns, bearer-companies, Colonial Horse, generals and their staffs, go plodding and jingling by in a procession that seems to be going on for ever. And beside and through them the long convoys of the different units, in heavy masses, come groaning and creaking along, the oxen sweating, the dust whirling, the naked Kaffirs yelling, and the long whips going like pistol-shots. The whole thing suggests more a national migration than the march of an army. And ever on the horizon hang new clouds of dust, and on distant slopes the scattered advance guards of new columns dribble into view. I fancy the Huns or the Goths, in one of their vast tribal invasions, may have moved like this. Or you might liken us to the dusty pilgrims on some great caravan route with Pretoria for our Mecca.

We crossed the Vaal at Lindiquies Drift, being now on the west flank, and met the Boers the day before yesterday two miles from here on the West Rand. The fight was a sharp one. They were in a strong position on some ridges, not steep, but with good cover among stones and rocks. We came at them from the west, having made a circuit. Our advance was hidden by the rolling of the ground, but the enemy guessed it, and sent a few shells at a venture, which came screaming along and buried themselves in the ground without doing much damage that I could see beyond knocking a Cape cart to pieces. By 2 P.M. we had crawled up the valley side and got several batteries of artillery where they could shell the Boer position. The two great "cow-guns," so called from the long teams of oxen that drag them, were hauled up the slope. The enemy got an inkling of our intention now, and his shells began to fall more adjacent. Then our fire began. It was difficult to see clearly. The dry grass of the veldt, which is always catching fire, was burning between us and the Boers; long lines of low smouldering fire, eating their way slowly along, and sending volumes of smoke drifting downward, obscuring the view. Half the ground was all black and charred where the fire had been; the rest white, dry grass. The Boer position was only about two miles from our ridge; a long shallow hollow of bare ground, without bush or rock, or any sort of cover on it, except a few anthills, separating us from them. Our field-batteries opened, and then the great five-inch cow-guns roared out. We ourselves were close to these with Hamilton (we are acting as his bodyguard), and with the other officers I crept up to the ridge and lay among the stones watching the whole show. After a shot or two all our guns got the range, a mere stone's throw for the great five-inchers. Their shrapnel burst along the rise, and we could see the hail of bullets after each explosion dusting the ground along the top where the Boers lay. The enemy answered very intermittently, mostly from their Long Tom far back, which our big guns kept feeling for. I never heard anything like the report of these big guns of ours and the shriek of the shells as they went on their way.

After the cannonade had been kept up for a bit, the infantry began their advance. This was, I think, the finest performance I have seen in the whole campaign. The Gordons did it; the Dargai battalion. They came up, line by line, behind our ridge and lay down along with us. Then, at the word "Advance," the front line got up and walked quietly down the slope, and away towards the opposite hill, walking in very open order, with gaps of about fifteen yards between the men. A moment or two would pass. Then when the front line had gone about fifty yards, the "Advance" would again be repeated, and another line of kilted men would lift themselves leisurely up and walk off. So on, line behind line, they went on their way, while we watched them, small dark figures clearly seen on the white grass, through our glasses with a painful interest. Before they had reached half way across, the vicious, dull

157

report, a sort of double *crick-crack*, of the Mausers began. Our guns were raining shrapnel along the enemy's position, shooting steady and fast to cover the Gordons' advance; but the Boers, especially when it comes to endurance, are dogged fellows. They see our infantry coming, and nothing will move them till they have had their shot. Soon we can see the little puffs of dust round the men, that mark where the bullets are striking. All the further side, up the long gradual slope to the Boer rocks, has been burnt black and bare, and the bullets, cutting through the cinders, throw up spots of dust, that show white against the black. Men here and there stagger and fall. It is hard to see whether they fall from being hit, or whether it is to shoot themselves. The fire gets faster and faster, our guns thunder, and through the drifting smoke of the veldt fires we can still see the Gordons moving onward. Then among the looking-out group, crouched near the guns, goes a little gasp and mutter of excitement. We catch on the black background, glistening in the sun, the quick twinkle of a number of little steel points. They are fixing bayonets! Now the little figures move quicker. They make for the left side of the ridge. A minute more, and along the sky-line we see them appear, a few at first, then more and more. They swing to the right, where the enemy's main position lies, and disappear. There is a sharp, rapid interchange of shots, and then the fire gradually lessens and dies away, and the position is captured. They have lost a hundred men in ten minutes, but they've done the trick.

Later on, Hamilton, one of the most beloved of our Generals, gallops forward, and on the hill they have won, as evening is closing, says a few words to the Gordons. "Men of the Gordons, officers of the Gordons, I want to tell you how proud I am of you; of my father's old regiment, and of the regiment I was born in. You have done splendidly. To-morrow all Scotland will be ringing with the news." This charge will, no doubt, take rank as one of the most brilliant things of the war.

Next morning at dawn, escorting the cow-guns, I came to where the Boers had held out so long among the scattered rocks. The Gordons were burying some of the Boer dead. There were several quite youngsters among them. One was a boy of not more than fourteen, I should think, like an English schoolboy. One of the Gordons there told me he saw him, during the advance, kneeling behind a stone and firing. He was shot through the forehead. There is something pathetic and infinitely disagreeable in finding these mere children opposed to one.

These infantry advances are the things that specially show up the courage of our troops. Each man, walking deliberately and by himself, is being individually shot at for the space of ten minutes or more, the bullets whistling past him or striking the ground near him. To walk steadily on through a fire of this sort, which gets momentarily hotter and better aimed as he diminishes the distance between himself and the enemy, in expectation every instant of knowing "what it feels like," is the highest test of courage that a soldier in these days can give. Nothing the mounted troops are, as a rule, called upon to perform comes near it. Knowing exactly from experience what lay in front of them, these Gordons were as cool as cucumbers. As they lay among the stones with us before beginning the advance, I spoke to several, answering their questions and pointing them out the lie of the ground and the Boer position. You could not have detected the least trace of anxiety or concern in any of them. The front rank, when the order to advance was given, stepped down with a swing of the kilt and a swagger that only a Highland regiment has. "Steady on the left;" they took their dressing as they reached the flat. Some one sang out, "When under fire wear a cheerful face;" and the men laughingly passed the word along, "When under fire wear a cheerful face."

PRETORIA
Pretoria, June 6, 1900

PRETORIA
Pretoria, June 6, 1900

It is generally considered rather a coup in war, I believe, to take the enemy's capital, isn't it? like taking a queen at chess. We keep on taking capitals, but I can't say it seems to make much difference. The Boers set no store by them apparently; neither Bloemfontein nor Pretoria have been seriously defended, and they go on fighting after their loss just as if nothing had happened.

For months Pretoria has been our beacon, and at first it seemed quite an impossibly long way off. Looked at from Bloemfontein, across 300 miles of dreary veldt and rugged kopjes and steep-banked rivers, and allowing for the machinations and devilments of ten or fifteen thousand Boers, our arrival here did seem a vague, indefinite, and far-off prospect. And yet in a day or two over the month here we are. Lord Roberts has brought us up in the most masterly way. He has moved with a big central column on the railway, while at the same time other columns, stretched far to right and left, moved parallel and threatened to outflank and enclose the enemy at every stand. So with wings beating and body steadily advancing, like some great kite or bird of prey, we have flapped our way northward.

Even here no stand was made. The town is strongly defended with several new forts, armed, we were told, with 10-inch guns, with a range of about twelve miles, which we supposed would put the noses of our poor cow-guns completely out of joint. The Boers had burnt the grass on all the hills to the south of the town, so that the blackened surface might show up the khaki uniform of our men, and offer a satisfactory mark, and things generally, as we slowly approached the tall black rampart of mountain south of Pretoria, seemed to point to a big engagement. But here, as so often elsewhere, it was borne in upon them that if they finally stayed and defended their capital, they would assuredly be surrounded and cut off; and so, though only at the last moment, we hear, they decided to leave. They put up an afternoon fight on the hills near the town, but this was only the work of a handful of men, probably intended to stave us off for a while while they finished their packing in Pretoria and got away. Lord Roberts got a battery up to the crest of a great big ridge, and we got a pompon up a still steeper one, and a vigorous cannonade was kept up and a good deal of rifle-fire indulged in till nearly dark. But this is often very deceptive. No doubt if it was the first battle you had been at, you would have put down the casualties, judging from the noise made, at several hundred. As a matter of fact, the peculiar thing about all this shooting is that, like the cursing in the Jackdaw of Rheims, "nobody seems one penny the worse." Loading is now so easy that it is not the slightest trouble to fire. The consequence is that a glimpse of a Boer's head on the sky-line a couple of miles off will find work for a battery of guns and a few score of rifles for the rest of the afternoon. About sunset time, when it begins to get cold, they will limber up and come away, and the report will go in that our shelling was very accurate, but that the enemy's loss could not be positively ascertained.

The day after the fight we made a triumphal procession through Pretoria, and marched past Lord Roberts and his staff, and all his generals and their staffs, assembled in the big square facing the Parliament House. We came along a long, straight street, with verandahed houses standing back in gardens, and trees partly shading the road, a ceaseless, slow, living river of khaki; solid blocks of infantry, with measured, even tread, the rifle barrels lightly rising and falling with the elastic, easy motion that sways them altogether as the men keep time; cavalry, regular and irregular, and, two by two, the rumbling guns. Mile after mile of this steady, deliberate, muddy tide that has crept so far, creeps on now through the Dutch capital. Look at the men! Through long exposure and the weeding out of the weak ones, they are now all picked men. The campaign has sorted them out, and every battalion is so much solid gristle and sinew. They show their condition in their lean, darkly-tanned faces; in the sinewy, blackened hands that grasp the rifle butts; in the way they carry themselves, with shoulders well back and heads erect, and in the easy, vigorous swing of their step.

I should like, while I am about it, to speak to you rather more at length about the British soldier. I should think my time spent on service, especially the five months in the ranks, time well spent, if only for the acquaintanceship it has brought with soldiers. In the field, on the march, in bivouac, I have met and associated and talked with them on equal terms. Under fire and in action I have watched them, have sat with them, long afternoons by rivers and under trees, and yarned with them on tramps in the blazing sun. Their language, habits, and character have to some extent grown familiar to me.

They are not, to begin with, a bit like the description I sometimes read of them in newspapers. In one of Kipling's books there is a description of a painting of a soldier in action; realistic and true to life; dirty and grimed and foul, with an assegai wound across the ankle, and the terror of death in his face. The dealer who took the picture made the artist alter it; had the uniform cleaned and the straps pipe-clayed, and the face smoothed and composed, and the ferocity and despair toned down to a plump and well-fed complacency, and made, in fact, all those alterations which were supposed to suit it to the public taste.

The newspapers describe the British soldier, I suppose, to suit the public too, much on the same lines. He is the most simpering, mild-mannered, and perfect gentleman. If you asked him to loot a farm, he would stare at you in shocked amazement. He is, of course, "as brave as a lion," his courage being always at that dead level of perfect heroism which makes the term quite meaningless. Except, however, when they are shining with the light of battle, his eyes regard all people, friends and foes alike, with an expression of kindness and brotherly love. He never uses a strong word, and under all circumstances the gentleness and sweet decorum of his manner is such as you would never expect to meet outside the Y.M.C.A.

This is about as much like our dear, old, real Tommy Atkins as Kipling's portrait was. Such a likeness does no honour to the man. It is simply lifeless. Whatever Tommy is, he is a man; not a round-eyed, pink-cheeked waxwork stuffed with bran. The truth is coarse and strong, but he can stand having the truth told about him.

Soldiers as a class (I take the town-bred, slum-bred majority, mind) are men who have discarded the civil standard of morality altogether. They simply ignore it. This, no doubt, is why civilians fight shy of them. In the game of life they don't play the same rules, and the consequence is a good deal of misunderstanding, until finally the civilian says he won't play with the Tommy any more. In soldiers' eyes lying, theft, drunkenness, bad language, &c., are not evils at all. They steal like jackdaws. No man's kit or belongings are safe for an instant in their neighbourhood unless under the owner's eye. To "lift" or "pinch" anything from anybody is one of the Tommy's ordinary everyday interests, a thing to be attended to and borne in mind along with his other daily cares and duties. Nothing is more common than to see some distracted private rushing about in search of a missing article, which he declares in anguished tones he has only just that instant laid down; his own agitation a marked contrast to the elaborate indifference of every one near him.

As to language, I used to think the language of a merchant ship's fo'c'sle pretty bad, but the language of Tommies in point of profanity quite equals, and in point of obscenity beats it hollow. This department is a speciality of his. Of course, after a little it becomes simply meaningless, and you scarcely notice it, but the haphazard and indiscriminate way, quite regardless of any meaning, in which he interlards ordinary sentences with beastly words, at first revolts you. Lying he treats with the same large charity. To lie like a trooper is quite a sound metaphor. He invents all sorts of elaborate lies for the mere pleasure of inventing them. He will come back from headquarters and tell you of the last despatch which he has just read with his own eyes (a victory or disaster, according to his mood at the moment), with all kinds of realistic details added; and you go and see for yourself, and there is no despatch at all. Looting, again, is one of his perpetual joys. Not merely looting for profit, though I have seen Tommies take possession of the most ridiculous things—perambulators and sewing machines, with a vague idea of carting them home somehow—but looting for the sheer fun of the destruction; tearing down pictures to kick their boots through them; smashing furniture for the fun of smashing it, and may be dressing up in women's clothes to finish with, and dancing among the ruins they have made. To pick up a good heavy stone and send it wallop right through the works of a piano is a great moment for Tommy. I daresay there is something in it, you know.

These are roughish traits, are they not? Sit down by this group of Tommies by the water-hole in the mid-day halt. They are filthy dirty, poor fellows. Their thin, khaki, sweat-stained uniforms are rotting on them. They have taken off tunics and shirts, and among the rags of flannel are searching for the lice which pester and annoy them. Here is a bit of raw humanity for you to study, a sample of the old Anglo-Saxon breed; what do you make of it? Are thieving, and lying, and looting, and bestial talk very bad things? If they are, Tommy is a bad man. But for some reason or other, since I got to know him, I have thought rather less of the iniquity of these things than I did before.

The day has been fearfully hot, as usual, and they have done a long march. They were up last night on picket, and have had nothing to eat all day as yet but a biscuit or two and a cup of milkless coffee. This sort of thing has been going on for months. They are tired and hungry and footsore. More than one falls back where he sits and drops into a sleep of utter exhaustion. But of any serious grumbling or discontent there is no sign. A few curse at the heat perhaps, but their hardships are mostly a subject for rough chaff and Cockney jokes. You thought you were roughing it a good deal, but look at the state these men are in. You gave yourself credit for some endurance, but look at their unaffected cheeriness. The whole army is the same. In their thousands, as you see them pass, the prevailing expression down all the swarthy faces is one of unfailing good-humour. They make no more of their hardships than Sandow of throwing about bars and bells that would crush an ordinary man flat. It dawns on one, the depth of manhood that is implied in endurance like this. "We sometimes get licked at first, but we mostly come out all right in the end." Tommy's good-natured face as he sweats it across the *veldt* gives some meaning to that boast.

In the crowds of his mates in the East End, in crowds of the unemployed and the like, you see the same temper—a sort of rough, good spirits, an indomitable, incorrigible cheerfulness that nothing, no outward misery, seems able to damp. In West End crowds (Hyde Park, for instance) you don't get this. There are smiles and laughs, as you look about at the faces, but they seem merely individual—one here, another there. In the crowd of roughs—though goodness knows there is little cause for merriment, so far as one can see—there is a quite different, deeper, and more universal feeling of bluff cheeriness, not put on, but unconscious, as though, in spite of present misery, things were going right for them somehow. I should say an East End crowd gave one a far deeper impression of animal spirits, of hope and cheeriness, than a West End one. And it is the same with soldiers. The officers are fine fellows, but in this point they yield to the soldiers.

And it means a lot. Of what use is even courage itself if it goes with impatience and a flash in the pan endurance? This quality of cheerfulness is really the quality that out-lasts all others. It means not only that you have an army in good fighting trim today, but that this time next year, or the year after, you will still have an army in good fighting trim. In the long-run it wears down all opposition, but it is not a characteristic you notice at first. Gradually it makes itself felt, and gradually it governs your estimate of the whole army. And then the peculiar wickedness of Tommy (a child's naughtiness for superficiality) ceases to offend you so much. Rather your own regulation code seems a trifle less important than it did. Let's all lie and steal; what does it signify? I would lie and steal till the crack of doom to gain the serene endurance of the British soldier.[1]

Of his courage one need scarcely speak. It is a subject on which a great deal of rubbish has been talked. It is not true that all soldiers are brave, nor is it true that even brave soldiers will go anywhere and do anything. On the other

---

1: This account is true of a type, but I should not let it stand if I thought it would make the reader forget that, besides these, there are any number of men in the army who lead lives in every way straight and honourable.

hand, it certainly is true that our soldiers' courage—that is, their apparent unconsciousness of danger—strikes one as very remarkable. You need not believe more about the light of battle and the warrior's lust, and all that sort of thing, than you want to. There is very little excitement in a modern battle, and the English soldier is not an excitable man, but this only makes the display of courage more striking. Nothing can be more terrible than one of our slow charges, a charge in which all the peril which used to be compressed into a hundred yards' rush in hot blood is spread out over an afternoon's walk. I am sure any man who has ever taken part in one of those ghastly processions, and, at thirty yards interval, watched the dust-spots, at first promiscuous, gradually concentrating round him, and listened to the constant soft whine or nearer hiss of passing bullets, and seen men fall and plodded on still, solitary, waiting his turn, would look upon the maddest and bloodiest rush of old days as a positive luxury by comparison.

What I think about our soldiers' courage is that it is of such a sort that it takes very little out of them. One of the foreign officers on Lord Roberts' staff, in a criticism in one of his own papers, has written that the English infantry, more than any he knows, has the knack of fighting and marching and keeping on at it, day after day, without getting stale or suffering from any reaction. The fact is, our Tommies go into a fight with much the same indifferent good-humour that they do everything else with. Towards the end of each day's march the soldiers all begin to look out for firewood, and if at that time you knock up against the enemy, you may see our infantry advancing to the attack with big logs tied to their backs and sticking up over their heads. Though it encumbers and bothers them and makes them much more conspicuous, not a Tommy will abandon his wood. Supper is a reality. The thought of being shot does not bother him. Men who fight like this can fight every day.

Taking him altogether, then, your general impression of the Tommy is one of solid good temper and strength. Of his faults and failings, when you get to know him, you cannot help making light; for his faults are faults of conduct only, while his strength is strength of character. As an individual, I daresay you could criticise him, but in the mass, for the strength of breed he shows and the confidence he gives you in your race, you will have nothing but admiration.

I have told you what I could about him, because he is a man you have never seen, and will probably never have a chance of seeing. For no one who has not seen Tommy in the field has seen him at all. If you love England, you must love the army. If you are a patriot, not merely a Jingo, the sight of these ragged battalions passing will give you such a thrill as only very fine and splendid things do give; and very proud you will feel if ever you have had a hand in sharing their work and been admitted to some sort of fellowship with them.

These are the lads who in their packed thousands tramped yesterday through Pretoria. Past old Kruger's house, a cottage you might almost call it, with its lions in front and several old burghers in black crying in the verandah, we went at a foot's pace, choking in the cloud of red dust, with the strains of "God Save the Queen" in our ears. We emerge into the square. The Volksraad is on our right; then the Grand Hotel, with all its windows full of English people, or sympathisers with England, many of them women, all waving handkerchiefs and raising a cracked cheer as we pass. I was staring at all this, whilst a big band on the right broke merrily out with the "Washington Post," and did not see till I almost brushed his horse's nose, our Commander-in-Chief standing like an amiable little statue at the head of all his generals and their staffs, with finger raised to helmet. It is quite a moment to remember, and I do really feel for an instant, what all the morning I have been trying to feel, that we are what literary people call "making history."

As for Pretoria itself, it is a pretty and well-wooded little place, with pink and white oleander trees in blossom, fir-trees, gums, and weeping-willows along the streams and round the little bungalow houses. The shady gardens and cool verandahs give these houses a very inviting air in this land of blazing sun. They have a comfortable, and at the same time sociable, look, the houses being near by each other, but each with a pretty garden and trees overhanging. Like all the works of these very practical people, the place is designed for convenience and comfort and not a bit for beauty. But the first two give it the last to some extent, give it a sort of simple and homely beauty of its own which is pleasing as far as it goes.

"Take heed to thyself, for the devil is unchained." We are told that Christian De Wet is loose again, and is trifling with our lines of communication. If this is so, our supplies will be cut off, the army will be starved, and you will never get this letter. There has been a pretty general hope that the taking of the capital would mean the end of the war. "We have fired our last shot," said some. At least we counted on a good rest. Alas! orders have just come in. Good-bye flowers and shady gardens and dreams of bottled beer and a dinner at the club. We march immediately.

Talking of soldiers, here is a soldier's story for you—

Officer (to distracted Tommy, fleeing for his life under shower of bullets): "Dash you! what the dash are you running for?"

Tommy, tearing on: "'Cause I ain't got no b—y wings."

Here's another—

First Tommy: "And the bullets was comin' that thick—"

Second Tommy: "Well, but 'adn't you got no ant'ills?"

First Tommy: "Ant'ills! Why, there wasn't ant'ills 'nough for the orficers."

THE MARCH SOUTH
Bethlehem, July 14, 1900

THE MARCH SOUTH
Bethlehem, July 14, 1900

Whenever in this campaign we have dealt the enemy what looked like a crushing blow, he has always hit back instantly at us. When Methuen reached the limit of his advance at the Modder River victory, the Boers were round immediately threatening us from behind. When we took Bloemfontein they at once swarmed round to the east and south, and dealt us two nasty blows at Sanna's Post and Reddersberg; and no sooner had we taken Pretoria than the same activity was displayed again.

They threatened us now from two points. Louis Botha had collected a large force, and was watching us from the hills east of the town, while the everlasting De Wet, far south, was breaking up the railway and burning our letters. The first thing we did, and we did it the very day after entering the capital, was to march against Botha. Ian Hamilton has paid our little corps the compliment of taking it on as his bodyguard. He is a general that inspires every one under him with great confidence. It is curious, by the way, how very soon troops get to know the worth of a leader; just as a pack of hounds knows by instinct when it is properly handled. Outsiders may argue about this or that general, and analyse his tactics, and never very likely get much nearer the truth (for there is a monstrous lot of luck one way or the other in all manoeuvres, and the ones often succeed that didn't ought to, and vice versa); but once you are under a man, you don't need to argue; you know. We all know that Ian Hamilton, with his pleasant well-bred manner, and the mutilated hand dangling as he rides, is the best man we have had over us yet, and we would all do great things to show our devotion.

The Diamond Hill action was one of those great big affairs which it would be impossible to explain without a plan of the country and a lot of little flags. Our attack from extreme left to right was spread over a frontage of, I daresay, twenty miles. The idea was for the mounted troops to turn the enemy's flanks and let in the infantry in front. Ian Hamilton had to deal with the Boer left flank, French with the right. Of course we saw and heard nothing of French, who might as well have been fighting in another planet, so far as we knew. Our difficulty here, as on some former occasions, was to find the limit of their flanks. The more we stretch out, the more they stretch out. They have the advantage of being all mounted, while the bulk of our force is infantry, massed inertly in the middle; and also from the lofty position they occupy they can command a bird's-eye view of the wide valley across which we are advancing, and perceive the disposition of our forces, and in what strength we are threatening the various points of defence, while their forces are quite concealed from us. This is so much in their favour that, on our flank at least, it is we, and not they, who are threatened with being outflanked.

Their position could scarcely have been stronger if nature had designed it for the purpose. A low range of hills gives admittance on the west side to a long wide valley, and on the east side of this a steep rocky range rises boldly up, showing in the sky a level outline like a rampart fringed with wall-like slabs of rock or detached masses, giving excellent cover from shrapnel. But besides this higher and last line of defence, there are some lower hills and slopes which project from the main rampart and command the valley, while they are in turn commanded by the heights. It is a two-step position, in fact. You carry the lower step first, and immediately come under the fire of the upper. The General told me next day that he thought it as strong as anything he had seen on the Natal side, and Winston Churchill set the matter at rest by pronouncing it stronger in point of formation than Spion Kop.

In the first day's fighting we drove them from the western hills and across the valley, which was more fertile than usual and full of cover, until we had forced them into the two-step eastern range. My own work lay right out on the flank end, at the very finger-tips, where the farthest limit of each force was trying to feel a way round the other. Here, with some of the Camerons, we felt about the hills, shelling them with a couple of guns for Boer sharpshooters, and occasionally flushing one or two. We were rather detached and out of the main action, feeling rather like a gun that has been sent to stop birds from "going back" while the main battue is at work in front. We stayed out all day, and as we rode in that night to headquarters the whole valley under the starlight was echoing like a great gallery and bustling with the multitude of our army arranging itself and settling down for the night. We picked our way through the various convoys hurrying forward in search of their brigades, but often losing their way or getting off the track, checked by muddy fords, where an engulfed team wallows piteously, barring the passage. We pass detachments of infantry hurrying in tired and silent, and meet other detachments with blankets and greatcoats coming out on picket. Waifs and strays, by ones and twos, who have lost their way, shout for guidance, hallooing dismally for the brigades or regiments to which they belong, and which many have small hope of rejoining that night. Meantime, right down the valley and far across it, the various camp-fires twinkle out like glow-worms. The air is keen and frosty, and stars, clear and sharp as icicles, glitter all over the sky. Above everything is still and calm, very well arranged evidently, and everything in its proper place. Below all is confusion, noise, and darkness, disappointment, and difficulty, vague wandering to and fro, lamentations, and general chaos. They manage these things better up there! However, after a bit order begins to reign. The several units draw together. The camp-fires are beacons. The waggons struggle up. The bleating of the lost sheep is gradually hushed, as one by one they find their way to their various folds, and slowly, in spite of darkness and broken ground, the tangle is smoothed out.

By a small farm, where the General lodges, blazes a huge fire. Round it gather some staff officers, and among them, recognised from afar, are the welcome tiger-skins of the Guides' officers. The Major sits by the blaze in that familiar attitude of his, like a witch in "Macbeth," with a wolf-skin karross drawn over his shoulders, and the firelight on his swarthy face as he turns it up with a grim laugh to chaff the others standing round. But there is rather a gloom on the party tonight. News has just come in that poor Airlie, charging at the head of his Lancers, has been killed. Many here knew him, and every one who knew him seems to have been fond of him.

Winston Churchill turns up and enlivens us. There are several colonels and senior officers squatting about, and Churchill takes the opportunity of giving them a bit of his mind. He is much annoyed with the day's proceedings. He has been a good deal shot at; so has the Duke, and so has the General. They have had to use their Mauser pistols. This sort of thing should not happen. Then where was French? Checked, indeed! a pretty fine thing! And the Guards? The Guards were somewhere where they had no business to be, instead of being somewhere else. Would any one kindly tell him why the Guards were not somewhere else? And Churchill (he has a face like a good-natured child, and looks about fourteen) eyes the old colonels, who fidget nervously round the fire like disturbed hens. He talks and argues incessantly, but very cleverly. Before he goes he dashes off a sketch of South Africa's future with a few words about farming and gold-mining. He gives us a cup of hot cocoa all round, which he produces from nowhere, like a conjuring trick, re-arranges our fire, tells us when the war will be over, and strolls off (daring the old colonels with his eye to so much as look at him) to the farm to give the General his final instructions about tomorrow's action.

Next day our infantry established itself on the lower step of the Boer position, but the final ridge still remained in their hands. It was a ding-dong fight between the two, for the positions were within half-rifle shot of each other. However, we could not turn them out, though we got a field-battery right up in the firing line, which cracked shrapnel over them as hard as ever it could load and fire. They had determined to hold that ridge till night gave them the opportunity of moving off their waggons and guns safely; and hold it they did. No doubt we could have carried it by storm, but crossing that thousand yards of open ground would have meant a terrible loss, and the General did not attempt it. As it was, there was a great deal of banging and blazing, almost like the old Modder days, for a time; guns hard at it, and Mausers and Lee-Metfords jabbering away at a great rate, though, as both sides were under cover, the loss was not heavy. The firing went on till pitch dark, and we camped close under the ridge we had won. Next morning we found the ridge vacant, with only heaps of empty cartridge cans and an occasional blood-stain on the rocks to show where our enemy had lain.

A little way out from Pretoria there are some very smart-looking new houses, what they call "villa residences" in England, built in the style, a sort of mild and tepid Gothic (what I call grocer's Gothic, for it always reminds me of brown sugar and arrowroot), common around watering-places; small gables sticking out everywhere, till it looks like a cluster of dog-kennels; walls faced with ornamental tiles and lath and plaster; small shrubberies round, and a name on the gate. There were two especially beautiful ones. The General had one and we had the other. Ours was quite new. There was no furniture in it; but this, as we had been so long without it, we did not miss. But everything we really needed—gorgeous wall-papers, and dados, and polished floors, and electric-bells, and stained-glass windows—was there. We had hot baths at the Grand Hotel, and we dined at the club, and we forgot all about the war, and the veldt, and the dust, and the long marches, and the Boer lurking in ambush, and the whispering bullet from the hill. This went on for two days, and then we marched again, and we have been marching ever since.

We left Pretoria on June 19th, and, taking it easy, reached Bethlehem on July 9th, doing a bit under 200 miles in the twenty days. The meaning of the new scheme begins to dawn on us. Clements and Paget have come up from the west; Rundle is down south-west, near Ficksburg; the Basuto border runs up from there south and south-east, and within the ground thus enclosed we have penned a very considerable force of the enemy, among whom is that Jack-in-the-box, Christian De Wet. We know they are there, and indeed we have little fights with their scouts every day. The question is, how are we to collar them? The country is very broken and hilly and very extensive.

Hunter is looking after us now. Poor Ian Hamilton, as you will know, had an accident at Heidelberg. His horse put a foot in an antbear's hole, just in front of me as it happened, and came down, flinging the general forward over his head. I thought he was killed, he lay so still, but it was only his collar-bone and a bad shaking. He is in the field again now.

Hunter has a great reputation as a fighter, which is rather

alarming, especially when we are confronted with such a poisonous country as the one before us now; a medley of big mountain ranges, fantastically heaped, stretching thirty miles south to Basutoland, and forming part of the great mountain formation that reaches to and culminates in the Drakensberg range. These hills are garrisoned by about 7000 Boers with several guns, and De Wet to lead them; altogether a formidable force. There is a saying, that you should not bite off more than you can chew. I hope we have not done that. Hunter looks as if he could chew a good lot, I think. Still the job is likely to be a difficult one to handle, and if he asks my advice I shall tell him to leave it to Rundle.

I should think a life of this sort would be likely to have some permanent effect on one's mind and intellect. The last mail—that is to say, the last news of any sort of the outside world—which we have received was on April 27th before leaving Bloemfontein; three months less a week since any whisper concerning events or people out of our immediate sight has reached us. My ignorance of things in general weighs on me. It is a taste of life in the dark ages before modern inventions kept one in touch with the world.

During all this time we have been wandering like an army in a dream over the unlimited surface of the veldt. The same programme is repeated day by day. A little before dawn you hear through your blanket-folds the first unwelcome "Saddle up," and the muttered curses in reply. You unwind yourself with groans. A white-frost fog blots out everything at fifty yards, and a white sugary frost encrusts the grass. These first hours are piercingly cold, for it is now mid-winter with us. A cup of water left overnight is frozen solid. You dress by simply drawing your revolver-strap over your shoulder, and flinging your blanket round you, make your way to where a couple of black boys are bending over the beginnings of a fire, and to which several other blanketed and shivering figures are converging with the same thought—coffee—in every mind.

Then the great army column that has curled itself up like a caterpillar for the night begins slowly to uncurl. On the march our huge convoy stretches out in line, waggon following waggon along the rude track, and extending to a length of nearly ten miles. At night, of course, it collects (parks is the proper word) at some selected spot where the ground is favourable, and where in the shape of a sluit, river, or farm-dam there is water. On the slopes and hills around infantry pickets are set, while the convoy and main camp are massed in the hollow beneath. You must not think of our camp in the English sense of the word. We have no tents. The men sleep tightly rolled in greatcoat and blanket, stretched on the bare earth, with saddles for pillows. If anything takes you about the camp at night, you might think you were walking among thick strewn corpses after a fearful carnage, so stiff and still the frosted bodies lie on the ground.

Now the great creature wakes for its next crawl. First its antennæ, or long feelers, are pushed out in front. Its scouts, that is, among which, if you belong to our corps, you will probably find yourself, go cantering on ahead. They pass the pickets on the hill, who promptly shoulder blankets and turn back to camp, and break into extended order, and throw out little feelers of their own in front and to the sides as they enter an unexplored country. Following them come several companies of infantry, a block of solid strength, marching at the top of the column, and a battery or section of guns. Then comes the long line of convoy waggons, piled high with provisions, fodder, and kit, strengthened and protected at intervals by companies of infantry marching at ease, with the two great cow-guns somewhere about the middle. The tail of the column, like the head, is strengthened by a considerable force of infantry, followed at an interval of a mile or so by the mounted rearguard, which has scattered its scouts far and wide across the track of the column, and withdraws them from point to point as we advance. Likewise to left and right, far out on the plain, the horsemen of the flank guards are scattered in little bands of twos and threes, cantering along or stopping and spying, sniffing cautiously round *kopjes* or peeping into farms, and by-and-by you will probably hear from one direction or other a few scattered single shots, and yonder two scouts in the distance, lately advancing so quietly, are now seen to be turned and galloping back as hard as they can split, while two or three Mausers crack at them from the sky-line.

It is a pretty sight, from some hill far in advance, to turn back and watch the army coming into view. You push on, scouts feeling the way, to occupy some prominent kopje on the line of march, and climbing up and sitting among the rocks, command with your glasses a view far and wide over the plain. The air has been very cold and sharp, with an intense penetrating cold hitherto, but now the sun is shining and its mellow warmth is instantly felt. The rich pure colour-lines, only seen when the sun, rising or setting, is low in the sky, lie straightly ruled across the plain, brown and orange and pale yellow, and in the distance blue. The ten-mile off rocks look but a mile in this air. Every object, distant or near, is exact to the least detail. So clear are the outlines you would think there was no atmosphere here at all, and that you might be looking out over the unaired landscapes of the moon. One would think that such an air would breed an exceptional race, and that the men, and horses too, for that matter, of this country would show something of the Arab character, sensitive, fiery, and high strung. Yet nothing can be conceived less Arab like than your stolid but practical Dutchman and the underbred screw he rides.

Left and right of you, your two or three flankers, half a

mile off, have halted, in obedience to your halting, and are standing by their horses' heads scanning the country. Under the *kopje* your main body are sitting about, while their ponies, with bridles thrown over their heads, graze. Far back, two or three miles, the bits of dark kilt showing behind their khaki aprons, a company of the Camerons comes into view, the brown colour so exactly matching the plain that they are first visible only by their motion. Here come the flank guards, sprinkled far out over the country. And now, at the point where the distant *kopjes* slope to the plain, the air grows heavy with dust-wreaths, rising like steam from a cauldron, and underneath, slowly emerging, comes something dark and solid. It is the head of the column. The great caterpillar is crawling forward. You must push on—"Stand to your horses!"

PRINSLOO'S SURRENDER—1
Camp, Near Fouriesberg, July 26, 1900

PRINSLOO'S SURRENDER—1
Camp, Near Fouriesberg, July 26, 1900

We have a whole day of peace and rest before us—very welcome after the hard fighting we have been doing lately. This lull is to allow Bruce-Hamilton and Macdonald to stop the exits at the eastern end of the valley. We don't want to push the enemy east till we are sure the passes in that direction have been secured. Some of us are annoyed at the delay. We were in touch with the enemy this morning, our scouts and advance guard exchanging shots with their rearguard. We could see them prancing about on the bare hills east of Fouriesberg, and making off in a leisurely way up the eastern valley, and most of us were quite expecting that we should give chase immediately.

Hunter rode forward to have a look. He watched the tiny horsemen hovering on the hills or cantering away; then back he came with a quiet smile on his face, and instead of ordering the advance, as the impetuous ones expected, he led his column back over the way we had come for several miles, and then camped.

So here we are, sitting or lying about, sleeping, smoking, or reading. Our camp is in a small plain, five or six miles from Fouriesberg, surrounded by ranges of great hills. Those south and east, their gaunt peaks rising, streaked with white, above the lower and nearer ones, are in Basutoland. They play an important part in our programme, for it is against that huge barrier that we are pressing the Boers. There are some rounded, turf-clad hills, but most are rocky. Sharp points and stony ridges rise up with jagged and clear-cut outlines into the sky, with gorges and valleys retreating in between, full of deep blue shade, and often horizontal bands of strata, showing like regularly built courses of white masonry along the flanks of the mountains. It is very fine, though gaunt, bare, and untenanted. We have had nothing but level veldt to march on for weeks past, and the change to the eye is a pleasant one. Nevertheless, it is a bad country for our business. To us mountain ranges are not fine scenery, but strong positions; and rocks and crags are not grand and picturesque, but merely good cover. We always serve out extra-ammunition when we come to a pretty bit of scenery.

The present position is this: We have got the Boers, a big lot of them, at any rate, into a very broken and mountainous country, a country which, though it suits their tactics and is strong for defence, is nevertheless very difficult to get out of. The way south is barred by the Basutoland border. They dare not cross that or they would have the hordes of Basutos, who are already buzzing and humming like a half-roused hive, on to them. The other passes Hunter occupies in this way: Rundle comes up from the south-west to Fouriesberg through Commando Nek. Paget and Clements march south towards the same point through Slabbert's Nek. A little farther east Hunter himself forces Retiefs Nek, while farther east still Bruce-Hamilton, helped by Macdonald, is to hold Naawpoort Nek and block the Golden Gate road. The western columns, i.e. Rundle's, Clement's, Paget's, and Hunter's, are to force a simultaneous entrance into the Fouriesberg valley, and having got the enemy's force jammed against the Basuto border, to force it to turn eastward up the rugged Caledon valley, the only two exits to which are, we hope, by this time held by Bruce-Hamilton and Macdonald. This we have now done. Now it only remains to see whether these eastern exits have been successfully occupied by our columns or not.

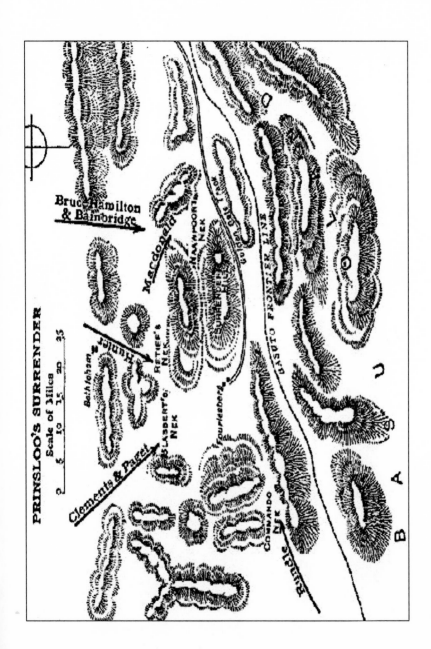

PRINSLOO'S SURRENDER

Scale of Miles

0 5 10 15 20 25

Bruce Hamilton & Bainbridge

Macdonald

Hunter

Bethlehem

Clements & Paget

Retief's NEK

Naauwpoort NEK

Surrender HILL

Slabert's NEK

Fouriesberg

Golden Gate Track

BASUTO FRONTIER LINE

Commando NEK

Rundle

Rundle NEK

B A S U T O

From the moment of leaving Bethlehem, at which place we remained nearly a fortnight while the General placed his columns, we entered among the hills and fighting was continuous. Our passage to force was Relief's Nek, and, as we had expected, the Boers made a determined stand there. The ground lay in a naturally defensive position; a narrow plain among steep, almost precipitous, ranges, and in the plain, arresting further progress, an abruptly sunken valley, scooped out to a depth of a couple of hundred feet; as though, what must perhaps have happened, some sudden collapse down below had allowed the ground here to fall in. The sides are in most places precipitous, but to the north they shelve up by degrees in terraces of sloping rock which a man can easily clamber up. The first terrace is only a few feet deep, and accordingly a number of men can form here along the brink and fire across the plain, being totally concealed from the advancing troops. Moreover, the edge of this curious and sudden valley is indented and pierced with a number of little crevices and fissures in which riflemen can snugly ensconce themselves with little risk of being seen by attackers in front. This was the main Boer position. You see it departed from the general rule, and instead of occupying a hill, occupied a hollow. They are past-masters in the art of choosing ground. The adjacent heights were also held.

On the morning of the 23rd we struck our camp a few miles north of the Nek, and advanced to find out whether the enemy were in position here or not. We started before daylight. The night had been intensely cold and very wet. On the high mountains snow had fallen. The sky was heavily clouded, and about sunrise-time dense masses of mist rose and clung about the hills, sometimes closing in the view at fifty yards and then drifting off and leaving it clear again. Our scouts advanced steadily, reconnoitring hill after hill and ridge after ridge, but still there was no sound of firing, and we began to think that the enemy had abandoned the place altogether. This preliminary scouting work, poking about in the hills with a handful of men to find the enemy, always reminds me of tufting for deer in the Exmoor woods before the pack is laid on.

Then there came a few shots from our extreme right, from the hills on the right of the valley's nose, sounding very muffled and dull in the mist, and we, out on the left, advanced with the more caution. It was my chance to come upon the enemy first on this side, and as it will give you a fair notion of the usual risks of scouting, I will tell you how it happened!

I was out with my tufters on the left front, and we were drawing with all possible care the hills on that side. In front of us was a tall peak, and I sent a few men to work round it on the left while I went round the right. This hill really overlooked the Boer position. My left flankers got round and rejoined me in front. Either they must have been concealed from the Boers by the mist or have been mistaken for a party of Boers themselves, for they had passed within a few hundred yards of the edge where the enemy lay and were not fired at.

Damant, our captain, coolest and bravest of officers, now joined me, and with two or three men we pushed cautiously on towards some loose rocks, which, from the top of the rise, seemed to command a view of the valley beneath. We had advanced to within eighty yards of the rocks, in open order, when we thought we heard voices talking, and immediately afterwards some one said loudly in Dutch, "Who rides there?" And then another voice more to the right exclaimed, "Here they are!" At the same instant one caught a motion as of heads and shoulders cuddling down and adjusting themselves in a disagreeable way. There they were and no mistake, all tucked in among the rocks like wood-lice.

Our position then was a curious one, for we had actually walked quite in the open up to within speaking distance of the main Boer position, a position that was to defy our army for a day and a half.

The ground sloped down in a slight hollow. It was thickly sprinkled with snow and dotted here and there with little green spots where the grass tufts showed through. A wire fence crossed the hollow lower down. Luckily we heard their voices before they started shooting, and instantly we turned and rode for it, the Mausers all opening immediately and the bullets cracking and whistling round our ears. As bad luck would have it, my pony, which, like most of them, knows and dreads the sound of rifles fired at him (though he will stand close to a battery or among men firing without minding it in the least), became so frantic at the noise of the bullets that I was quite unable to steer him. With head wrenched round he bored away straight down the hill towards the wire. As we got to it I managed to lift him half round and we struck it sideways. The shock flung me forward on to his neck, which I clasped with my left arm and just saved myself falling. For an instant or two he struggled in the wire, a mark for every rifle, and then got clear. In his efforts he had got half through his girths and the saddle was back on his rump. A pretty spectacle we must have looked, I sitting back on his tail, my hat in my hand, both stirrups dangling, and the bullets whistling round both of us like hailstones. However, I lugged him out at last, and we went up the side of the fence broadside on to the shooters, as hard as ever we could lay legs to the ground. It is a difficult thing to bring off a crossing shot at that pace, and in a few hundred yards we were over the slope and out of shot. I have seen lots of our men have much narrower escapes than this.

Well, after all that, we will get back to the action. Having located the enemy, the Guides all collected behind the con-

193

ical hill, climbed up, and from the edges of it began shooting down into the Boer position. Here we were joined by the Black Watch, who carried on the same game. It was not, however, at all a paying game, and the fact that the Boers had not held this hill themselves, though so close to their position, is sufficient of itself to show their remarkable skill in choice of ground. For the hill, conical and regular in shape, was perfectly bare, and while they behind the sharp ledges and in the fissures of the rocks below were well concealed from the men above, these as they crept round the smooth hillside came into immediate view against the sky. The sleet of bullets shaving the hill edge was like the wind whistling past. The Black Watch lost a lot of men here. In the afternoon the Guides and some of Lovat's Scouts pushed forward on the left and gained a low ridge, where, lying down, we could command a part of the enemy's position, and send in a flanking fire. This manoeuvre was useful and suggested a plan for next day. That night I had to take out a picket on a hill on our south-east front and had but a sorry time of it; for it was a bitterly cold, rather wet night, and the position was not without its anxiety. I got little sleep.

Next morning, July 24, soon after light, the main body of the Guides and Lovat's Scouts (who are under Rimington at present) came out, and we rode down to the slopes on the left of the Boer valley again. Here we crept up as far as we could and began to put in our fire. It must have been very annoying for them, for a part of their position was quite exposed to us. We could see the short white cliff at the edge of the basin and the Boers moving about and running up and down, diving into fissures and getting under cover, for all the world like rabbits, as our fire searched the position. They replied, but though a lot of bullets were whistling about, no one was hit. There was a Maxim at the foot of the conical hill rattling away, and the Black Watch were again on the hill itself, blazing away at the rocks as

194

vigorously as ever. Then at last between us and them up gallops a section of guns, and the little puff balls begin to burst along the rock edge in a way which we could see was very disconcerting for the Boers, who were rapidly finding the place too hot for them. A little after, some one sings out, "Here comes the attack!" and true enough we can make out the little khaki dots in long loose strings moving forward round the hill towards the valley head. It is the Seaforths. We on our side "carry on the motion," dash forward, lie down and shoot, and on again. We make for a *kopje* on our edge of the valley. The fire is too hot for the Boers to dare to show up much and there is not much opposition. But I can assure you that a charge of 1500 yards, even without the enemy's fire, is a serious thing enough. Puffing and panting, I struggle on. Long-legged Colonials go striding by land leave me gasping in the rear. When at last we reach the *kopje* and look down into the sunken valley, the Seaforths are pouring in their fire on the retreating Boers, our fellows are doing the same from the *kopje* top, but I myself am too pumped out to care for anything and can only lie on the ground and gasp.

I see in your last letter you want to know about the character of the Guides, and whether there has been any cases of treachery among them. I don't know what started these old yarns. They were invented about Magersfontein time, probably to account for that awful mishap, and got into the local press here and made a lot of fuss, but we have heard nothing since on that score. There is such a lot of treachery put here (owing to the intermingling of English and Dutch in their two territories) that almost anything in that line seems credible, and there are numbers of people about, loafers in bars and fifth-rate boarding-houses, to whom anything base seems perfectly natural, and who delight in starting and circulating such tales. At the same time there are also numbers of honest and loyal men, and it is from these, and exclusively from these, that the fighters are drawn. In South Africa, and among the South Africans, a war of this sort, between neighbours and cousins, is the sternest test of loyalty. Many have failed to stand it. But the loyalty of those who have not wavered, but have taken up arms for their country in a quarrel like this, is of a sort you can trust to the utmost extremity. There are no men in the field who feel so deep an animosity towards the Boers, and whom the Boers in their turn hate so much, as the fighting South African Colonials. As for the Guides, I can assure you that there has not been a single case of any one of our men having been accused of treachery, nor suspected of treachery. I have made careful inquiries, lest such a case might have occurred without my knowledge, and I am assured by our adjutant (C.H. Rankin, Captain 7th Hussars) that there has been no such case, and that the slander was without the slightest foundation whatever.

Shortly after Magersfontein the greater part of the Guides turned back to Colesberg, leaving fifteen of us with Methuen, the services of the whole corps not being required, as Methuen's force was now stationary. Before it left, Methuen paraded the corps and spoke in the warmest terms of the good work it had done. Nevertheless it was their turning back, or being sent back, as it was called, that gave a pretext to the slander that was then started. Later, when his attention was called to the story, Methuen wrote to the *Cape Times* a most emphatic letter vindicating the corps from the least suspicion, and indignantly denying that the least cause for any had existed. Lord Roberts himself, who came up soon afterwards, wrote a very handsome and decisive letter to the same paper, and since then I don't think we have heard anything about it. The whole story is so ridiculous, considering the way the Guides hate the Boers, and the danger of the services they do, that to any one who knows anything about the corps it is a tale rather to be laughed, at than seriously resented. I saw the other day a letter from Hunter to Rimington, in which the General speaks of the corps with a kind of weighty deliberation that is very satisfactory, mentioning emphatically its "trustworthiness," its "bravery," and its "exceptional and proved value in the field."

Our casualty list so far is about forty per cent., I believe; but this loss, though not light, does not in a Colonial corps give an adequate idea of the service done. All the Colonials, so far as I know (the Australians and South Africans certainly), have much the same qualities that make our enemies so formidable. They have individual intelligence and skill, a faculty for observation, and the habit of thinking for themselves. They are therefore able to take care of themselves in a way which our regular troops, mostly town-bred men, without independent training, cannot do.

The difference comes out chiefly in scouting, including all the flanking and advance guard business, extending for several miles to left and right, and in front and rear of an army column, by which that column feels its way through an enemy's country. The regulars usually carry out these tactics in long lines with wide intervals between the men. But nothing is so conspicuous as a long line of men riding at fifty yards' interval. They can be detected a dozen miles off, and plenty of opportunities will occur for a mobile, cunning enemy like the Boers to lie in ambush and get a shot at the outsider.

Our regulars are better at this game than they used to be, but many lives have been lost at it. On the other hand, Colonials adopt more the tactics of a Scotch gillie in a deer forest, whose object is to see, but not to be seen. Sky-lines are avoided and cover taken every advantage of. From places where a good view is to be obtained the country is intently studied; not by a horseman poised in relief like the Achilles statue in Hyde Park, but by a man who has left his horse on the reverse slope and lies hidden among the rocks with his glass. Again, if a farm or suspicious-looking *kopje* has to be approached, this is partly encircled, and threatened or examined in flank or rear before being occupied; while if the place, a long range of hills for instance, has to be approached in front, a sudden left or right wheel at long range may often draw the enemy's fire. These are a few of the many expedients that sometimes suggest themselves to lessen risk.

In all, the first necessity is personal intelligence in the men and the habit of taking notice and thinking for themselves, faculties which the independent, self-reliant life of the Colonials has greatly developed. Just the same holds good when it comes to shooting; choosing cover, keeping oneself hidden, creeping on from point to point without giving the enemy a fair shot, or detecting the probable bushes or rocks behind which an enemy may be lying, or any sign of his whereabouts.

The Tommy as he advances is apt to expose himself, because he doesn't think. The Colonial will get to the same spot perhaps quite unperceived. This is why I say that our loss does not give an adequate idea of the work done by the corps. The defence of the conical hill here at Relief's Nek is a good example. Our men hold the hill for several hours before the regulars come up, and lose one man. As soon as the regulars arrive (though by this time the exposed places are known and the enemy located), they begin to lose men, and by the conclusion of the action have lost, I am told, over forty.

I think, and have often spoken so highly of our soldiers' courage, that I don't hesitate to point out their weakness. They are lacking in personal intelligence. For all their pluck, they don't know how to look after themselves. There have been, as you will have heard, many cases in which detached parties of our cavalry, mounted infantry, and yeomanry have been cut off and captured. How often has this happened to the Colonials?

PRINSLOO'S SURRENDER—2

August 4th

PRINSLOO'S SURRENDER—2
August 4th

We have been up the valley and back again, and I write this once more from Fouriesberg. We passed through here, joining Rundle, as I told you a week ago, and pushed on eastward in the direction of Naawpoort Nek and the Golden Gate. Six miles out from here, passing through a very rugged country, we came on their outposts. These we shelled and drove back. They then retired to some hills not very high, but with perpendicular sides of low white cliffs commanding the approach across the plain. These they held till nightfall. We shelled them a good deal and knocked out the only gun they had, and the infantry pushed forward in front and we took a hill on the right, but the attack was not pressed home, as it would have cost too many lives. The infantry took the hill during the night, but found it evacuated, the Boers having retired as soon as it got dark.

We did not know all this time how things had gone with Macdonald and Bruce-Hamilton, and whether or not they had been able to block the eastern exits. On this everything depended. So it was with a feeling of the most gleeful satisfaction that we heard next morning, having followed the Boers up some two or three miles without seeing anything of them, the deep, heavy baying of a big gun in the distance, which we all recognised as the voice of one of the 5-inch cow-guns that had gone with Bruce-Hamilton. It fired a few shots and then ceased. With infinite toil, forty oxen to each gun, we then dragged our own two 5-inchers up the hill we were on, and got them into position for shelling the defiles ahead. They were not, however, needed. Messengers now began to arrive from the Boer *laagers* carrying white flags. There was a lot of palaver. These went, others came. Le Gallais, our chief of the staff, interviewed them, while Hunter strolled a little way apart, dreamily admiring the view. It was evident the Boer envoys were sticking out for terms which they couldn't get. I could see Le Gallais indicate the surroundings with summary gestures. The Boers looked very glum. They eyed the cow-guns especially with profound disgust. These were looking particularly ridiculous. The nose of one of them projected in the direction of those secret Boer-tenanted defiles as if the great creature were sniffing for its enemies in the distance; which gave it a very truculent and threatening air, as who should say, "Come now, Le Gallais, old fellow, suppose you let me put a word in," while the other, hanging its head till its nose touched the very ground, seemed overcome, poor wretch, with a sudden fit of bashfulness, most absurd in so huge and warlike a monster. The Boers looked from them to Le Gallais and from Le Gallais to them, but there was no more hope from one than the other, and at last they realised that there was nothing for it but to surrender, and surrender was agreed to. We could scarcely believe our good fortune. At Paardeberg we caught 4000, but we used 50,000, more or less, to do it, and we lost about 1500 doing it. Here we trapped as many or more, composed of some of the best commandoes of the Free State, caught them, too, in a wild mountainous country such as you would think was almost impregnable. We used 15,000 to do it, and we lost, I suppose, not 200 altogether. Also, we have taken enormous quantities of horses, oxen, and waggons, which will come in very useful.

It seems to me that Hunter deserves the utmost credit that can be given to him. We have had plenty of generals who have done direct fighting and done it well; but, with the doubtful exception of Paardeberg, we have had no triumph of tactics. We have never scored off the Boers, never made a big capture, or cut them up, or taken guns or transport, or bested them in any decisive way by superior strategy till now. This has always been our lament. We have always said, "Why, with all these armies in the field, cannot we surround them, or catch them, or deal a decisive blow of some sort?" But hitherto we have never succeeded in bringing off such a coup. We have pushed them before us, losing as many or more than they at every shift, but, whenever we have thought to get a hold of them, they have always eluded us. You may think it is a strange thing that they have been caught this time. The daring of Hunter's plan and the rapidity it was carried out with made it succeed. The Boers—so they tell me at least—never believed that we should venture with so small a force to penetrate by four or five different routes into such a strong country. The scheme seemed to lay us open to a disaster if the enemy had rapidly concentrated and flung itself on one of the separated forces. This danger, however, was more apparent than real, because the ground manoeuvred over was not altogether of very large extent, so that relief might be sent from one column to another, or the enemy, if concentrated against one column, rapidly followed up by one or more of the others. Besides which, if the country offered strong positions to take, it offered strong ones to hold, and in a very short time any threatened column could have placed itself in such a position as to make it impossible for the Boers to shift it in the time at their disposal. Still the plan, considering the Boers' skill in defending strong positions, had an audacious look about it. Several of the Boer prisoners have since told me—I don't know with what truth—that they thought we should follow them in by the Relief Nek pass, and that it was their intention to work round and threaten our communications, and either cut us off or force us to fight our way out as best we could.

The quickness of our advance, too, was of the utmost importance. From the moment we started, the enemy was given no opportunity to pull himself together and look about him. Hunter, Paget, Clements, and Rundle dashed into the Fouriesberg Valley exactly together. Directly we had got through, Hunter detached the main part of his column, the Highland Brigade, under Macdonald, and sent it with several guns as hard as it could pelt to back up Bruce-Hamilton, knowing, now that we had carried our end of the valley, that the pressure would come at the east end. Meantime, while Macdonald marched, we waited. We even retreated two or three miles, and for twenty-four hours lay on the pass and slept. Then we got up and began sauntering up the big irregular valley along the Basutoland border towards Naawpoort Nek.

It was a moment of infinite expectation. Bets were laid on the amount of our bag. The general impression was that we should get some of them, but that the main body would, somehow or other, escape. We had so often toiled and taken nothing, that this sudden miraculous draught quite flabbergasted us. And what must have been the feelings of the poor Boers? They tried Naawpoort Nek: no exit. They knocked at the Golden Gate: it was locked. Then back they turned and met Hunter sauntering up the valley, and we gave them the time of day with our cow-guns, and told them how glad we were to see them. "Fancy meeting you, of all people in the world!" And so they chucked it. It was a complete checkmate.

The surrender occupied the next three days; our total bag 4100, I am told. I wish you could have been there. It was a memorable sight among those uninhabited and lonely mountains. The heights of Basutoland, ridge behind ridge, to right of us; the tops snow streaked; groups of excited Basutos riding about in the plains, watching our movements; to left the great mountain chain we had fought our way through; and in the midst spread over the wide saddle-backed hill, that slopes away north-eastward, and breaks up in a throng of sharp peaks and a jumble of inaccessible-looking hills in the direction of the Golden Gate, is drawn up the dirty, ragged, healthy, sun-scorched British army with greasy rifles in its blackened hands, watching imperturbably and without much interest, the parties of Boers, and waggons, and droves of cattle as they come meandering in.

Each Boer, as he rides up, hands over his rifle, or more often flings it angrily on the ground, and the armourers set to work, smashing them all across an anvil. Rather a waste of good weapons it seemed, I must say. Many of the Boers were quite boys, about fourteen or fifteen. They are much better looking than you would think from the men. The men are big and well built, but they look, for the most part, stupid and loutish, and when this is not so, their expression is more often cunning than intelligent. The amount of hair about their face, too, and their indifference to washing, does not improve their appearance.

However, in the boy stage, and before the dulness of their surrounding has had time to tell, they are quite different, frank-faced and manly, with clear skin, tall and well grown, like young larches. It does seem strange that such mere children should be in the field against us. What would you think of giving Puckie a rifle and sending him out to fight? Boer prisoners have told me that the courage of these boys could be relied on; they were often braver, and would stick to a position they had been placed in longer than the men.

They showed traces of the experience they had been through, though. Not only in being deeply tanned and more or less ragged and thin, but by an unmistakable expression (in many instances) in their faces and in their eyes; a dilated look, as of one who sees something appalling before him, and braces himself to face it out. Considering what it is to be exposed to lyddite and shrapnel fire (the absolute hell of din and concussion besides rain of bullets), one doesn't wonder that it leaves marks on young faces.

R. and I rode eastward through the hills in the Golden Gate direction, meeting parties of Boers, waggons, Cape-carts, &c., coming straggling in. It reminded me of the road to Epsom on a Derby morning. There is some pleasure in meeting Boers on these terms. "Good morning. How are you? A pleasant morning for a ride, is it not?" "Good morning, sir; it is fine now, but I think we shall have rain later." That's what I like. There's nothing like a little urbanity.

Towards the end of a long valley we come to some signs of defensive work that interest us. The Boers evidently expected to be able to await our advance here before they found their retreat was cut off. They have thrown up some shelters. We noticed from afar off several very conspicuous stone sangars, but coming close, we were surprised to find that they were made of stones loosely put together with big chinks, very flimsy and frail, and much too high for their purpose, too.

They evidently were not intended for shelters at all. What were they there for? We looked carefully round, and at last the meaning of the device struck us. A hundred yards to the right the ground dropped sharp, leaving an edge; here was the real position and the natural cover. We walked over, and found the usual little hollows and inconspicuous stones arranged. Here was where their riflemen had lain, with a view right up the valley. And the meaning of those conspicuous edifices was now plain. Stuck up on the bare brow, plain to be seen at 2000 yards, they were simply meant to draw our fire. The smokeless Mausers would have told no tales, and I have no doubt that, if the attack had come off, the device would have more or less succeeded, for the stone shelters, though obviously dummies on close inspection, looked all right at a distance. Besides, a definite mark always attracts fire. It was characteristic of Boer cuteness.

FIGHTING & TREKKING
Heilbron, August 17

FIGHTING & TREKKING
Heilbron, August 17

We stayed several days among the mountains on the scene of the surrender, collecting our prisoners and the waggons, guns, horses, &c., and sending them off to the railway. The valley, viewed from the hill where we were camped, looked much like one of our West Country horse fairs on a very large scale. The separate commandoes were herded together in big groups of several hundred men, sitting and lying about and talking. The ox-waggons and battered Cape-carts were drawn up together in a great array; but the busiest part of it all was the division of the horses into mobs fit or unfit for remounts, and the distribution of them to the various regiments. Rimington superintended this job. Of course, after all our marching, we were sadly in want of remounts. The Boers had any number of horses, many of them bringing in two or three apiece, and the majority were in good condition and fit for work, probably owing to the fact that the grazing all about this side of the Free State, especially among these mountains, is excellent. The South African ponies, I may tell you, are the only satisfactory mounts for South Africa. We have tried horses from all parts of the world now, and they can none of them stand the climate, work, and food like the native breeds. The South African pony, wretched little brute as he looks, will tripple and amble on, week after week and month after month, with a heavy man on his back, and nothing to eat but the pickings of sour, dried-up veldt grass and an occasional handful of Indian corn; and though you will eye him with an eye of scorn, no doubt (if he should happen to be allotted to your use), and envy some other man his fat Burmese or Argentine, yet by-and-by you will find out your mistake; for the fat Burmese and the Argentine, and all the other imported breeds, will gradually languish and fade away, and droop and die, worn down by the unremitting work and the bad, insufficient food; but your ragged little South African will still amble on, still hump himself for his saddle in the morning, and still, whenever you dismount, poke about for roots and fibres of withered grass as tough as himself, or make an occasional hearty meal off the straw coverings of a case of whisky bottles. With an action that gives the least possible exertion; with the digestion of an ostrich, and the eye of a pariah dog for any stray morsel of food; with an extraordinary capacity for taking rest in snatches, and recouping himself by a roll whenever you take his saddle off; and of course, from the natural tough-ness of his constitution, too, he is able to stand the long and gradual strain of being many hours under the saddle every day (and perhaps part of the night, too) in a way that unac-customed horses cannot do. By this time we all know his merits, and there is immense demand from every mounted corps for the Boer ponies. The Major is up to his eyes in work, as officers and orderlies come galloping up with req-uisitions from the various regiments. He has the born horse lover's dislike for parting with a really good horse except to a man he knows something about. Loud and uproarious is the chaff and protestations (now dropping to confidential mutterings) as the herds of horses are broken up and the various lots assigned. As I say, it looks from the hilltop ex-actly like a west country fair on an enlarged scale, and the great lonely Basuto mountains, too, might seem a larger edition of the Exmoor hills around Winsford. The Boer prisoners, poor fellows, have no eye for the picturesque.

They congregate together and grumble and watch the distribution of their horses with a very sour expression.

From this point we sent our prisoners in, viá Winberg, to the railway, the Major and most of the corps going with them as part of the escort; while I with twenty men, consisting partly of Guides and partly of Lovat's Scouts, was detached to continue as bodyguard to Hunter. He, with the main column (we reunited at Bethlehem), marched to Lindley and then here to Heilbron.

It was ten miles south of this that we came in contact with Olivier. Olivier and De Wet had both broken through our cordon at different times and escaped from the hills. Sent one morning with a message to the Sussex outside Slabbert's Nek I saw shells bursting, and all the appearance of a heavy fight going on over the hills to the north-west. This was Christian De Wet, who with several guns and about 1500 well-mounted men, had made a dash for freedom when he found the place was getting too hot, and had been promptly tackled by Broadwood when he got outside. Pursuer and pursued vanished into the blue distance of the veldt, battering each other as they went, like birds that fight and fly at the same time. Broadwood, however, had got hold of his enemy by the wrong end. What happened exactly we don't know, but De Wet got clear somehow, and immediately turned his attention to his beloved railway line, which he never can tear himself away from for more than a few days at a time. He is now, I should imagine, in the very seventh heaven of delight, having torn up miles of it, besides capturing several trains.

De Wet is getting an immense reputation. The rapidity of his movements is extraordinary. He always has two or three of our columns after him; sometimes half-a-dozen. Among these he wings his way like a fowl of some different breed, a hawk among owls. Some amusement was caused by the report in orders the other day that De Wet had marched north pursued "by various generals;" as if two or three, more or less, didn't matter, as indeed it didn't. Of course, mere fast marching would not always extricate him, but he shows such marvellous coolness and common sense in the way in which he doubles. Several times he has been reported surrounded; but each time when we came to look he had disappeared. It is like a conjuring trick. He seems to have an intuitive knowledge of the plans of our generals, and to divine how any movements of his will modify theirs. He makes a swift march. This he knows will set in motion a certain column. Night comes and back he steals, and dashes out through the gap left without any one being the wiser. He never loses his *sangfroid*, but acts always, in the most hopeless positions, with equal craft and rapidity. In short, like the prophet Isaiah, he is *capable de tout*. For he can hit hard, too. I think since the arrival of the main army he is the only man who has scored off us at all freely. Sanna's Post and Reddersberg came first; then, last May, came the capture of the 500 Yeomanry at Lindley; that was followed immediately by the surprise of the Heilbron convoy and all its escort; then came the capture of the Derbyshire Militia, and a few days later the taking of Roodeval with a train of mails and various details. Even when he had bolted out the other day between our legs, and was flying north with two or three cavalry brigades after him, he found time to snap up a hundred Welsh Fusiliers and break the line as he passed. He is, they say, extremely amusing, and keeps his men always in a good temper with his jests; the other day, after one of his many train captures, he sent a message to the base to say that "he was sufficiently supplied with stores now, and would they kindly send up some remounts." He is now the only prize left worth taking, and every one is desperately keen in his pursuit. I notice, however, that people never seem to meet him when they want to, though when they don't want to, they very often do.

Olivier, with a force about equal to De Wet, also broke out from the hills, and having reached the open country, hung about to watch our movements. There are some *kopjes* ten miles south of Heilbron, very nicely arranged, with a back hill commanding a front one, so that the first position gained would only bring us under the fire of the second; a very favourite Boer trick. Here Olivier awaited our coming, and, knowing the range to an inch, landed his first shell plump in the middle of our convoy. Hunter, and we with him (it is certainly great fun being with the Staff for the time being), were at the head of the column, and heard the shell go over. Never have I seen a better shot. It exploded on the track, right underneath a great waggon, to the amazement and consternation of the Kaffir drivers and the wretched oxen; though they were all, I believe, a good deal more frightened than hurt. Three or four more quickly followed. "Roll that up," said Le Gallais to the Guide carrying the General's flag. A few minutes passed, during which we were shot at without being able to reply. Then two Field Batteries came galloping to the front. Guns! Guns! Way for the guns! like the fire-engines down Piccadilly they came tearing along. As the iron wheels strike upon rocks the guns leap and swing. Stones and splinters fly right and left, and the dust flung up by wheel and hoof boils along their course. Nothing is more stirring than to see guns coming full speed into action. In another minute they have lined up on the ridge and their shells are bursting on the enemy's hill.

Hector Macdonald is a man who always amuses me. Ordinarily he is a somewhat grim-looking individual; but when there is any fighting going on his whole manner changes, and he beams and mantles with a sort of suppressed mirth. He comes swaggering up now as the guns are opening, looking like a man who has just been told the best story he ever heard in his life, and is still chuckling over it. "They're on to us again," he bubbles out, knocking

215

his boot with his whip in irrepressible glee. "What! what! they're on to us again." He looks round at us and grins, and seems to lick his lips as a shell goes howling overhead and bursts behind us. His merits as a general are very much discussed, but there is one thing he does thoroughly enjoy, more than any man I know, and that is being shot at. I suppose he would rather win a battle than lose one, but I am sure he would rather lose one than not fight at all.

Next to him, in marked contrast to his excitement, stands out the cool attentive face of "Archie" Hunter; the most popular officer, as I believe one might call him, of all the British army. He is noted chiefly as a fighter and for his dash and gallantry. He did all the fighting in the Egyptian campaign. During the siege of Ladysmith it was he who planned and led the night attack which blew up the big Boer gun. When I was coming out on the steamer the one question asked among the war correspondents, who wanted to be where the most fighting was going on, was "Where will Hunter be?" But it is probably his kindness and the deep interest he feels in all his men that makes him so universally popular. Here is a tiny instance, perhaps not worth mentioning. We were halted on the march for a moment, sitting about and smoking, when the General gave the word to mount, and one of the orderlies, a trooper of the Lancers, jumped up in a hurry and left his pipe behind him. Hunter saw the filthy, precious object lying on the ground, and put it in his own pocket. At the next halt he went up to the trooper, and with that manner of his of deliberate kindness, returned it to him. A mere nothing, of course, but very characteristic.

He has a way of looking at you, no matter who you are, Tommy or officer or what not, with a wonderfully kind expression, as if he felt the most friendly interest in you. And so he does; it is not a bit put on. He does not seem to think about himself, but about the people and things round him. Every morning he finds time to stop and ask after the horses and men of our little body, and to exchange a word with one or two of the men whom he has had occasion to notice. Not a grain of condescension is there in him; not even a thought that he is giving them pleasure. It is a natural impulse with him, the result of the real regard and interest he feels in every soldier that marches under him. In action his manner, always calm, is just as calm as at any other time. He says little; observing the most important developments or listening to the reports of orderlies from various parts of the field, more often than not without any comment at all. Yet nothing escapes him.

Our action with Olivier is a rather stupid one, and I shall not attempt to describe it. We take the first position, losing from forty to fifty men, only to find that the enemy have retired to the second range, and that it is too late to follow them up. Probably the only man at all satisfied with the day's performance is old Mac.

Through a weary land we have come marching north these ten days. The *veldt* is at its worst, parched and dry and dead. Our column trekking raises a huge cloud of reddish dust that hangs still in the air, and marks for miles back the way we have come. The whole expanse is quite colourless—almost white, or a dirty grey. All day long the blue sky is unvaried, and the sun glares down unobscured by a cloud; sky and earth emphasising each other's dull monotony. Only at sunrise and late evening some richer and purer lines of colour lie across the distant plain, and the air is fresh and keen. Round about the town, which, like all these Boer towns, stuck down in the middle of the *veldt*, reminds one of some moonstruck flotilla becalmed on a distant sea, the grass is all worn and eaten to the very dust. Whiffs of horrid smell from dead carcases of horses and cattle taint the air. All the water consists of a feeble stream, stagnant now and reduced to a line of muddy pools, some reserved for horses, some for washing, and some for drinking, but all of the same mud colour.

And yet even for this country, I think it with a kind of dull surprise as I look out over the naked hideousness of the land, men can be found to fight. What is it to be a child of the *veldt*, and never to have known any other life except the life of these plains? It is to reproduce in your own nature the main features of this extraordinary scenery. Here is a life of absolute monotony, a landscape, huge, and on a grand scale, but dull and unvaried, and quite destitute of any kind of interest, of any noteworthy detail, of any feature that excites attention and remark. And the people, its children, are like unto it. Their minds are as blank, as totally devoid of culture and of ideas as the plains around them. They have an infinite capacity for existing without doing anything or thinking anything; in a state of physical and mental inertia that would drive an Englishman mad. A Boer farmer, sitting on his stoep, large and strong, but absolutely lethargic, is the very incarnation of the spirit of the *veldt*. At the same time, when one remembers the clatter and gabble of our civilisation, it is impossible to deny him a certain dignity, though it may be only the dignity of cattle.

The problem will apparently be, when we have burnt these people out or shot them, and in various ways annexed a good deal of the land they now live on, how are we to replace them? What strikes one is that time and the country, acting on the naturally phlegmatic Dutch character, has produced a type exactly suited to this life and these surroundings. And it does seem in many ways a pity to destroy this type unless you have something to take its place. Except in one or two very limited areas, accessible to markets, and where there is a water supply, no English colonist would care to settle in this country. The Canadians and Australians, many of whom volunteered, and came here with the view of having a look at the land and perhaps settling, are, I hear, unanimous in condemning it. Indeed, it does not require any great knowledge of agriculture to see that a country like this, a lofty table-land, dry and barren, with no market handy, or chance of irrigation, is a wretched poor farming country. Hence the pity it seems of wiping out the burghers. They may not be a very lofty type of humanity, but they had the advantage in nature's scheme of filling a niche which no one else, when they are turned out, will care to fill in their place. The old dead-alive farm, the sunny stoep, the few flocks and herds and wandering horses sparsely scattered over the barren plain, the huge ox-waggon, most characteristic and intimate of their possessions, part tent and part conveyance, formed for the slow but sure navigation of these solitudes, and reminding one a great deal of the rough but seaworthy smacks and luggers of our coasts, that somehow seem in their rudeness and efficiency to stand for the very character of a whole life, all these things are no doubt infinitely dear to the Boer farmer, and make up for him the only life possible, but I don't think it would be a possible life for any one else. It seems inevitable that large numbers of farms, owing to death of owners, war indemnity claims, bankruptcy, and utter ruin of present holders, &c., will fall into the hands of our Government when the war is over, and these will be especially the poorer farms. But yet probably as years pass they will tend to lapse once more into Dutch hands, for it is difficult to believe that men of our race will ever submit to such a life of absolute stagnation. In dealing with the future of the country, it will always be a point that will have to be borne in mind, that the natural conditions of life outside the towns are such as favour the Dutch character very much more than they do the English.

WRITTEN FROM HOSPITAL
Hospital, Kronstadt, September 6, 1900

WRITTEN FROM HOSPITAL
Hospital, Kronstadt, September 6, 1900

It is only a bad attack of influenza. I lie here in a dim, brown holland coloured twilight. A large marquee of double folded canvas keeps out the sun; a few shafts of light twinkle through here and there. Through three entrance gaps I catch glimpses, crossed by a web of tent ropes, of other surrounding tents, each neatly enclosed by a border of whitened stones, the purpose of which is to prevent people at night from tripping over the ropes. Everything is scrupulously neat and clean. Orderlies run from tent to tent minding their patients. Every now and then a pretty little nursing sister, with white cuffs and scarlet pelisse, trips across the open spaces between the straight lines of marquees, or stops to have a moment's chat and a little quiet bit of a flirt (they can always find time for that, I notice) with one of the officers or doctors. I watch with faint interest and a feeling of vague recollection. She looks up sideways and shades the sun off her eyes with her fingers. They keep it up still then!

Some way off, among the Tommies' quarters, I can see groups of patients in clean, dark-blue clothes walking about, or sitting on seats, taking the air; some hobbling on crutches, some with arms in slings, heads bandaged, or patched and mended in some way or other. You feel like some damaged implement tossed aside a moment for repair. "Mend me this lieutenant!" The doctors get to work, deft and quick; a little strengthening, repairing, polishing, and out you are shot again.

It has been the only glimpse of absolute peace and rest I have had this eleven months. Every one is kind and sympathetic; a cool breeze blows through the looped-up tents; it is all very luxurious and pleasant for wearied-out soldiers. I like to lie and watch the little pictures through the tent openings of low blue *veldt* hills in the distance (which somehow remind one of the background glimpses in old Italian pictures), and dream over things one has seen and done, many of which seem already such ages ago, and listen to the bugle calls that sound at intervals in the camp. I have managed to buy some pyjamas. Probably you would see something very ludicrous in the way in which, after an elaborate hot-bath and hair-cutting, dressed out in one's clean pyjamas and lying between clean sheets, one rolls one's eyes with unutterable complacency on one's surroundings. All our comforts are attended to. We have a shell-proof shelter in a ravine close by, handy in case of visits from De Wet; and the two great cow-guns, like guardian angels, doze on the top of the hill behind the hospital. Under the shadow of their wing I always feel perfectly safe.

From patients who come in daily from various parts of the country and various columns we get a general impression of how things are going. The army seems to be adopting very severe measures to try and end the campaign out of hand, and the papers at home are loudly calling for such measures, I see, and justifying them. Nevertheless, it is childish to pretend that it is a crime in the Boers to continue fighting, or that they have done anything to disentitle them to the usages of civilised warfare. The various columns that are now marching about the country are carrying on the work of destruction pretty indiscriminately, and we have burnt and destroyed by now many scores of farms. Ruin, with great hardship and want, which may ultimately border on starvation, must be the result to many families. These measures are not likely, I am afraid, to conduce much to the united South Africa we talk so much of and thought we were fighting for.

I had to go myself the other day, at the General's bidding, to burn a farm near the line of march. We got to the place, and I gave the inmates, three women and some children, ten minutes to clear their clothes and things out of the house, and my men then fetched bundles of straw and we proceeded to burn it down. The old grandmother was very angry. She told me that, though I was making a fine blaze now, it was nothing compared to the flames that I myself should be consumed in hereafter. Most of them, however, were too miserable to curse. The women cried and the children stood by holding on to them and looking with large frightened eyes at the burning house. They won't forget that sight, I'll bet a sovereign, not even when they grow up. We rode away and left them, a forlorn little group, standing among their household goods—beds, furniture, and gimcracks strewn about the *veldt*; the crackling of the fire in their ears, and smoke and flame streaming overhead. The worst moment is when you first come to the house. The people thought we had called for refreshments, and one of the women went to get milk. Then we had to tell them that we had come to burn the place down. I simply didn't know which way to look. One of the women's husbands had been killed at Magersfontein. There were others, men and boys, away fighting; whether dead or alive they did not know.

I give you this as a sample of what is going on pretty generally. Our troops are everywhere at work burning and laying waste, and enormous reserves of famine and misery are being laid up for these countries in the future.

How far do you mean to go in this? Are you going to burn down every house, and turn the whole country into a desert? I don't think it can be done. You can't carry out the Cromwellian method in the nineteenth century. Too many people know what is going on, and consciences are too tender. On the other hand, nothing is so disastrous as that method half carried out. We can't exterminate the Dutch or seriously reduce their numbers. We can do enough to make hatred of England and thirst for revenge the first duty of every Dutchman, and we can't effectively reduce the numbers of the men who will carry that duty out. Of course it is not a question of the war only. It is a question of governing the country afterwards.

So far we only really hold the ground on which our armies stand. If I were to walk out from this tent a mile or two over the hills yonder, I should probably be shot. Kronstadt has been ours for four months. It is on the main railway. The country all round is being repeatedly crossed by our troops. Yet an Englishman would not be safe for a minute out of range of those guns on the hill.

There is a delightful feeling of spring in the air. We have had some warm, heavy rains lately. The veldt grass, till now dry and dusty and almost white, is beginning to push up tiny green blades, and the green colour is beginning to spread almost imperceptibly over the distant hills. I begin to feel a sort of kindred impulse in myself. The old lethargy, bred of the dull, monotonous marches over the dreary plains, is passing, and I begin to cock an attentive eye at the signs of awakening, and feel that I am waking up myself. If you could see the view from here, the barren expanse of veldt stretching miles away, the cluster of tin roofs and the few leafless thorn-trees beyond, I have no doubt you would laugh at this fancy of a spring day. And yet I am sure I can feel it; there is a change in the air. It has grown elastic and feels alive, and there is a smell in it to my mind of earth and vegetables. Yesterday, when I toddled in as far as the village, I saw a little fruit tree in a garden that carried white starry blossoms at the ends of its black twigs. It gave me quite a thrill. Oh, to be in England now that April—Dear me! I was forgetting 'tis autumn, and partridges and stubble fields with you.

The Hospital Commission of Inquiry has just turned up here, very dignified and grand in a train of half-a-dozen saloon carriages, which must be a great nuisance on the overworked lines. I have had several talks with the R.A.M.C. officers and men here about the alleged neglect and deficiencies, especially with the second in command, a very candid, liberal-minded man. He quite admits the shortcomings. The service is under-manned. There are not enough medical officers and not enough orderlies. This hospital, for instance, is entitled to a full colonel and two lieutenant-colonels, instead of which it has only one lieutenant-colonel, and the same proportion is preserved in the lower grades. Men in all departments are stinted, and the hospitals are all seriously short-handed. They have done their best to make up the deficiency with volunteers and civilian doctors and surgeons, but it is only partly made up. Their numbers compare very unfavourably with the numbers allotted to other nations' hospitals in the field. This has all been represented to the War Office many times of late years without result.

At the same time, with the men and accommodation they had, the hospitals have done their utmost. In the base hospitals there was nothing to complain of. At Bloemfontein there was great suffering owing to lack of medical staff, surgeons, nurses, orderlies, &c., and also owing to the lack of necessary supplies and medical comforts. For the shortness of the staff the War Office is of course responsible, and as blaming the War Office hurts nobody, I dare say the Commission will come down on it severely. For the shortness of supplies, this was due to the working of our line of communication, which considered the efficiency of the army a great deal, and the lives of the sick very little. But here you come to individuals, and the matter craves careful handling.

It is no fun fighting for you people at home, because you don't know when to clap. The English papers' account of Prinsloo's surrender have just come in. By Jupiter, for all the notice you take of it, it might be the capture of a Boer picket and a dozen men. Here have we been marching and fighting and freezing and sweating and climbing up great Alpine mountains in the snow for weeks, and captured 4000 great ugly live Boers and all their guns and baggage, and by the god of war, you hardly take the trouble to say thank you. This sort of thing will just suit Hunter, because his idea of bliss is to do the work and run the risk, and then somehow to evade the praise. But he ought not to be allowed to evade it. It is true we had no war correspondents with us, but I should have thought the bare facts would have spoken for themselves. It was the first thing of the war and our one really big score off the Boers. However, I shall not discuss it any more. I am disgusted with you. Mafeking day is about your form.

FIGHTING & FARM BURNING
Frankfort, November 23, 1900

FIGHTING & FARM BURNING
Frankfort, November 23, 1900

Frankfort is one of our small garrison towns. It exists in a perpetual state of siege, like Heilbron, Lindley, Ladybrand, Winberg, Bethlehem, and a dozen others in this neighbourhood; in fact, like all the towns held by us not on the railway. At intervals of a month or two a column comes along bringing supplies and news from the outside world; mails, papers, parcels, clothes and kit, great quantities of regular rations, ammunition, &c., &c. You can imagine how eagerly the little garrison, stranded for months in this aching desolation, looks for the column's coming. Then arise other questions. Sometimes a part of the garrison is relieved and receives orders to join the column, while some of the troops forming the column are left behind in their place. Of course every one in the town is longing to get away, and every one in the column is dreading having to stay, and there is an interval of ghastly expectation while contradictory rumours go hurtling from village to camp and back again; and men look at each other like cannibals, every one hoping the doom will fall on some one else. We in our corps are spared all this anxiety, and can lie on our backs and look on and condole with the unlucky ones. We never get left anywhere.

For the last few weeks we have been cruising about over the *veldt* from one little British fort to another with our huge fleet of waggons, doling out supplies. During this time we have been fighting more or less, I think, every day.

Perhaps you would hardly call it fighting; long-range sniping the greater part of it. Out of our 250 mounted men we have had some half-dozen casualties only, and we have accounted for a dozen or so of the enemy and a few prisoners. They have the advantage of their intimate knowledge of the country. We have the advantage of a pompom and two 15-pounders. These are invaluable in keeping the Boers at a respectful distance. It is rather satisfactory to plump some shrapnel on to a group of waiting, watching Boers three miles off, who are just concocting in their sinful hearts some scheme for getting a shot at you; or to lay a necklace of exploding pompom shells among some rocks where you guess they are hiding. "There, my boys, take that, and I hope you enjoy it," I feel inclined to say. You will understand that the side that has no guns at this game is apt to look rather silly. Rimington has initiated an entirely new use for guns. They are used now with the Scouts. Instead of remaining with the column, where they would never be of the slightest use, he takes them right out to the limits of his flankers or advance or rear guard, or wherever there is most need of them. So that when these scattered skirmishers get engaged, as they are constantly doing, instead of having to extricate themselves as they best can from an awkward corner, and being followed up and hampered and pressed as they keep up with the column, they know that in about two minutes they will hear the voice of one of the 15-pounders or the indignant pompom speaking on their behalf, and that the pressure will be immediately relieved. I am sure that the use made of these guns has saved us a number of casualties, besides inflicting loss on the enemy. It isn't very orthodox, I fancy, and I have noticed officers of the column rather stare sometimes at the sight of these volatile guns of ours careering away in the distance, but with the Colonel this is only another reason for using them so. At the same time the pertinacity of these Dutchmen is really remarkable, and the instant the guns limber up, on they come, darting round corners and creeping upon us with a zeal that never seems to diminish.

The work falls chiefly on front and rear guards, but perhaps mainly on the rear, as the difficulty of retiring is usually greater than advancing; i.e., if the advance guard gets pressed, all they have to do is to sit tight and the natural advance of the column will bring them up supports. But when the rear guard gets engaged, the advance of the main column tends to leave it stranded; it is bound to keep on retiring to avoid this, and retiring under fire is a difficult and dangerous job. The Boers, who have an instinctive knowledge how to make themselves most disagreeable, of course know all about this susceptibility of a rearguard, and there are always sure to be a number of them sniffing about in that direction. "Where are you today?" "Rearguard." "Oh! Good-bye, then!" was the farewell given to a rearguard officer this morning.

On the other hand, the advance is of course the most exciting. You make a dash for a *kopje*, probably uncertain if it is held or not. The clucking of the old Mausers at long range warns you that it is, and a few bullets kick the dust up. The squadron swing to the right to flank the kopje, and the fire gets hotter and the whistle of bullets sharper and closer. Suddenly the welcome report of a gun, followed by a second one, sounds behind you, and next instant the rush of the quick-coming shells is heard overhead. Then the squadron goes headlong for the *kopje*. The ponies tear along, mad with excitement, their hoofs thundering on the hard ground. The men grip their loaded carbines with their right hands; not one that won't be first if he can. There go the shells! There is a little shout of approval; one bursts right among the rocks on the top of the *kopje* in a puff of white smoke; the other half-way down, raising a great cloud of dust. The Mauser fire ceases as if by magic, and the next instant the racing squadron has reached the rise. Down jump the riders and clamber up over the stones. Yonder the enemy go, bundling along a rough track not 500 yards away, half seen through whirling dust. The men fling themselves down, some tearing a handful of cartridges from their bandoliers to have handy, and settle their carbines on the rocks. *Crack!* goes the first shot, and at the sound, as at a signal, the covey of fleeing Boers shakes out and scatters over the veldt. The fire quickens rapidly as the carbines come into action. Every Boer as he rides off, you can see through the glasses, is pursued and attended by little dust tufts that tell where the bullets strike. Surely they can't be going to get off scot-free. "Take your time, men; now do take your time," insists our captain. "A thousand yards, and aim well ahead!" And now at last it is seen with glee that something is the matter with the man on the white horse. Horse is it, or man? Both apparently. The man seems to be lying on his horse's neck, and the horse has lapsed into a walk. Instantly two of his comrades have turned to him. One begins thrashing the horse with his rifle into a canter. The other seems to be holding the rider in the saddle. Every carbine is on to them. Another Boer jumps off and lies down, and the report of his rifle reaches us at the same instant that a bullet whistles overhead. No one attends to him. Every man is blazing away at the little slow moving group of three, a good mark even at this distance. But it is not to be; though the dust spots are all round them, hit them we can't; and at last as they move away in the distance, the last reluctant shot is fired, and we give it up. On this particular occasion we capture one of the Boers a little further on hidden in a farm garden, his horse having been shot, though we did not notice it. This accounts for two anyway, which is about what we expect, and we proceed good-naturedly to help the farm people out with some of their furniture before burning the house down.

I am writing this lying on my back in our tiny tent. Outside the sun is blazing. Across the river, on the edge of the hill, our picket, under the lee of a *kraal* wall, is shooting at intervals. It sounds as if some one in the distance were chopping wood. The Colonel and Driscoll are standing just outside watching through their glasses. They can make out Boer scouts on the horizon, but no one pays much attention.

Driscoll, of Driscoll's Scouts, is a thick-set, sinewy man, rather short than tall. He is of an absolute sooty blackness. Hair and moustache coal-black, and complexion so scorched and swarthy that at a little distance you might almost take him for a nigger. There is about his face a look of unmistakable determination amounting to ferocity in moments of excitement. He looks and is a born fighter, but is apt to be over headlong in action. His scouts are part of our 250 mounted men under Rimington.

As for the Colonel I don't know if I have ever tried to describe him to you. He is a man who invites description. Of all the men in the army he is the one you would single out to sketch. An artist would be at him at once. He is the living image of what one imagines Brian de Bois Guilbert to have been. An inch or two over six feet high, his figure, spare but lengthy and muscular, has been so knocked about (by hunting and polo accidents) that it has rather a lopsided look, and he leans slightly to one side as he walks, but this does not interfere with his strength and activity nor detract from the distinguished and particularly graceful look of the man. His face, like Driscoll's, is sun-blackened rather than sun-browned; its general expression stern and grim, and when he is thinking and talking about the Boers (he talks about them just as Bois Guilbert did about the Saracens) this expression deepens into something positively savage, and he looks, and can perhaps sometimes be, a relentless enemy. But this is only half the man. In ordinary talk he is quite different. He has the Celtic sensitiveness and humour. He is an artist. His manner among friends is extraordinarily winning and sympathetic, and his grave melancholy face has a way of breaking into a most infectious laugh. Altogether, what with his tall person, dark determined face, his fierceness and gentleness, and the general air of the devil about him, you are not surprised to find that no soldier's name is more common in men's mouths out here than Mike Rimington's. You might fit Marmion's lines to him well enough—

His square-turned joints and length of limb
Show him no carpet knight so trim,
But in close fight a warrior grim.

He ought to have lived five hundred years ago and dressed in chain-mail and led out his lances to plunder and foray. As it is he does his best even in the nineteenth century. Picturesque is the word that best describes him. He makes every one else look hopelessly commonplace. His men admire him immensely, like him a good deal, and fear him a little. Generals in command sometimes find him, I fancy, a bit of a handful, that is, if their policy is at all a backward one. But most people watch him and talk of him with a certain interest, and whatever their opinions or ideas of him may be, one feels sure that none who have once met will easily forget him.

He is essentially a man who means business, who believes that the army is here to fight, and it is especially in action that he makes his value felt. Then, when he leads his squadron and the rifles begin to speak, and the first few shots come one by one like the first drops of a shower, and when he turns round in his saddle and thunders his, "Let them go" down the ranks, then I tell you there is not a trooper at his heels who does not realise that the man at their head is the right man in the right place.

At the same time it would be a mistake to think of him as one of our "let me get at them," all sword and spurs officers. There have been several of this sort in the army, and it is impossible to help very often admiring their dash. But they are most dangerous leaders. What chiefly distinguishes the Boers is their coolness. You cannot bluff or flurry them, or shift them by the impetuosity of your attack from a position which they are strong enough to hold. If indeed you have reason to believe them weak, then the faster you go at them the better: for if they mean going this will force them to go in a hurry and you will diminish the time you are under fire. But see your calculations are pretty sound, for if they don't mean bolting it will not be the fury of your charge that will make them. Generally when they begin on you at a very long range it is safe to go for them; but if they reserve their fire then look out for squalls. The Colonel has a very cool judgment in these matters; and though no one, when he does go for them, goes straighter and faster than he, no one, on the other hand, calculates more coolly the probable effect and consequence of the move.

In all scouting operations in our frequent long patrols he shows the same mixture of prudence and daring. He goes long distances from his supports and penetrates far into the enemy's country, and yet in none of these expeditions has he ever got trapped or cut off. Of course with men like the Guides, who have experience of the country and the enemy, and ways of picking up information not open to strangers, this is easier than it would be with men who had no such experience; but at the same time the chief credit and responsibility in these affairs must rest with the commanding officer. For one thing Rimington has an extraordinary good eye for a country. Perhaps at first you will scarcely realise the value of this gift. The features of this country and the way the long, undulating slopes of the veldt merge into each other are extremely perplexing, and as an engagement may be carried on over many miles of ground and your own movements may be extensive and involved, it becomes very difficult, in fact to most people absolutely impossible, to remember the lie of the land and how the various hills and slopes are related to each other. Thinking about it and trying to observe does no good at all; but some people have an extraordinary instinct by which they hold the configuration of the ground mapped in their head; judging not by slow calculation and an effort of the memory, but intuitively and at once. This instinct is called "an eye for a country," and is a most valuable gift. Personally, I am very ill equipped with it, which makes me the more inclined perhaps to admire it in others. It is developed in the Colonel to an extraordinary degree, and is one of the chief means by which, however hard beset, he has always been able, so far, to find a way out. Most nearly of any of our officers his tactics in daring and in craft resemble the tactics of that prince of scouting officers, Christian De Wet.

Kronstadt, Lindley, Heilbron, Frankfort, has been our round so far. We now turn westward along the south of the Vaal. Farm burning goes merrily on, and our course through the country is marked as in prehistoric ages, by pillars of smoke by day and fire by night. We usually burn from six to a dozen farms a day; these being about all that in this sparsely-inhabited country we encounter. I do not gather that any special reason or cause is alleged or proved against the farms burnt. If Boers have used the farm; if the owner is on commando; if the line within a certain distance has been blown up; or even if there are Boers in the neighbourhood who persist in fighting—these are some of the reasons. Of course the people living in the farms have no say in these matters, and are quite powerless to interfere with the plans of the fighting Boers. Anyway we find that one reason or other generally covers pretty nearly every farm we come to, and so to save trouble we burn the lot without inquiry; unless, indeed, which sometimes happens, some names are given in before marching in the morning of farms to be spared.

The men belonging to the farm are always away and only the women left. Of these there are often three or four generations; grandmother, mother, and family of girls. The boys over thirteen or fourteen are usually fighting with their papas. The people are disconcertingly like English, especially the girls and children—fair and big and healthy looking. These folk we invite out on to the veldt or into the little garden in front, where they huddle together in their cotton frocks and big cotton sun-bonnets, while our men set fire to the house. Sometimes they entreat that it may be spared, and once or twice in an agony of rage they have invoked curses on our heads. But this is quite the exception. As a rule they make no sign, and simply look on and say nothing. One young woman in a farm yesterday, which I think she had not started life long in, went into a fit of hysterics when she saw the flames breaking out, and finally fainted away.

I wish I had my camera. Unfortunately it got damaged, and I have not been able to take any photographs. These farms would make a good subject. They are dry and burn well. The fire bursts out of windows and doors with a loud roaring, and black volumes of smoke roll overhead. Standing round are a dozen or two of men holding horses. The women, in a little group, cling together, comforting each other or hiding their faces in each other's laps. In the background a number of Tommies are seen chasing poultry, flinging stones, and throwing themselves prostrate on maimed chickens and ducks, whose melancholy squawks fill the air. Further off still, herds and flocks and horses are being collected and driven off, while, on the top of the nearest high ground, a party of men, rifles in hand, guard against a surprise from the enemy, a few of whom can generally be seen in the distance watching the destruction of their homes.

One hears the women talk. Their ideas about the war are peculiar, for they all maintain that they will succeed in the long-run in asserting their independence, and seem to think that things are going quite satisfactorily for them. "Of course we shall go on fighting," they say, quite with surprise. "How long?" "Oh, as long as may be necessary. Till you go away." It is curious coming to household after household and finding the whole lot of them, women and children, so unanimous, so agreed in the spirit in which they face their afflictions. Husbands and sons in the hill fighting. Homes in the valley blazing, and they sitting and watching it all, almost always with the same fortitude, the same patience, and the same resolve. I am impressed, for I have never seen anything of the sort before. It is not often in these days that you see one big, simple, primitive instinct, like love of country, acting on a whole people at once. Many of our officers, the thoughtful and candid-minded ones, do these people justice; but many don't. Many catch at any explanation but the true one, and attribute every kind of motive save the only one that will explain the facts. They refuse to call the Boers patriots, but that the Boers are prepared to face a slow extermination in defence of their country is now evident. It has become more evident since the war has assumed its present character of individual, personal effort. I much respect and admire them for it.

It is time to bring this long letter to an end. I wish I could see an end to the campaign. When I come home "an old, old, aged and infirm old man," I mean to pass the evening of my days in a quiet cottage with its full allowance of honeysuckle and roses. There I shall grow sweet williams and, if I can stand the extra excitement, perhaps keep a pig. They tell me the Times has pronounced the war over. I would be glad to pay £5 out of my own pocket to have the man who wrote that out here on the *veldt* with us for a week. We have just heard that Dewetsdorp has fallen, and that there is a rising in the Colony near Aliwal North. *Vogue la galère!*

THE SITUATION
Camp on the Vaal, Klerksdorp, December 23, 1900

THE SITUATION
Camp on the Vaal, Klerksdorp, December 23, 1900

We are encamped close to the Vaal, which is here a fine stream, as wide as the Thames at Richmond. I have just been bathing in it. It is early morning, and I am sitting under a thicket of great weeping willows by the river. The banks slope down and make a trough for the stream a good deal below the level of the plain, and in this hollow, hidden till you are close to it, congregates all the verdure there is for miles, especially a quantity of willow trees, with gnarled black trunks leaning down to the stream, sometimes bending over and burying themselves in the ground and then shooting up again, making arches and long vistas, with green grass below and silvery foliage waving above. After our long marches on the *veldt*, the contrast here is wonderfully refreshing. One seems to drink in the coolness and greenness of the scene with eyes that have grown thirsty for such things. The trees straddling down the bank are rather like figures of men, giants that have flung themselves down, resting on hands and elbows, delighted, one would think, as I am, to come and rest near water again.

I can hardly believe that it only wants two days to Christmas. Our last Christmas we spent on the Modder. I remember it well; a wet night, and all night long we sat on a steep kopje watching the lights of a Boer *laager* and expecting to be attacked. Methuen's little campaign strikes one now as a sort of prelude, or overture, to the main show; but how very much surprised we should have been that November morning when we marched from Orange River Camp if you had told us we should ever be looked at in that light. Ten thousand men was a big army in those days.

We have been on the trek now for about six weeks with Bruce-Hamilton, and though we have not so far been seriously engaged, there has been almost daily fighting round the fringes and skirts of the column ("skirt-fighting," you may call it).

> "November 17.—Left Lindley. This neighbourhood quite as disturbed as ever. Shooting.
>
> "November 18.—More shooting. Boers in all hills.
>
> "November 19.—More shooting and galloping about. Reached Heilbron.
>
> "November 20.—Left for Frankfort. Boers in attendance as usual. Our two guns and pompom very useful."

Those were the last entries I made in my diary. The day's events became too monotonous to chronicle, but very much the same sort of entries would have applied to almost every day since. Sometimes there are exciting incidents. Yesterday half-a-dozen Boers hid in a little hollow which just concealed them until our column came along, and opened fire at close range on the flank guard. One or two men were hit and several horses. My friend Vice had five bullets through his horse and was not touched himself, which was rather lucky for him (or unlucky for the horse). A few days before that we were camped on the river and had a picket on the other side. Two or three Boers crept up the river right between our picket and the main body, and then walked straight to the picket as if coming from us and fired into it at point-blank range. They mortally wounded one of our men and in the dusk escaped. They are as cunning as Indians. Sometimes, as in these cases, they show great coolness and daring, while at others they are easily dispersed; but they are generally pretty keen, and you have to be very much on the alert in dealing with them.

You at home will probably be annoyed to find the war dragging on so. About election time the papers were announcing that it was over. It had been a hard job, they said, but it was finished at last. A good deal was occurring out here which did not quite tally with that theory, but those things were ignored or very slightly referred to, so that we on the spot wondered to see the war drop out of sight, and were puzzled to read in *The Times* that only a few desperadoes remained in the field just at the time that two commandoes were invading the Colony, another raiding Natal, a garrison and two guns captured at Dewetsdorp, and the line blown up in ten different places. The continuance of the war must strike you as a renewal, but there was never a lull really.

People who think the war can be ended by farm-burning, &c., mistake the Boer temper. I scarcely know how to convey to you any idea of the spirit of determination that exists among them all, women and even children as well as men. The other day I picked up at a farmhouse a short characteristic form of prayer, written out evidently by the wife in a child's copybook, ending thus: "Forgive me all my sins for the sake of your Son Jesus Christ, in whom I put all my trust for days of sorrow and pain. And bring back my dear husband and child and brothers, and give us our land back again, which we paid for with blood from the beginning." Simple enough as you see, and no particular cant about it, but very much in earnest. At another farm a small girl interrupted her preparation for departure to play indignantly their national anthem at us on an old piano. We were carting the people off. It was raining hard and blowing—a miserable, hurried home-leaving; ransacked house, muddy soldiers, a distracted mother saving one or two trifles and pushing along her children to the ox-waggon out-side, and this poor little wretch in the midst of it all pulling herself together to strum a final defiance. One smiled, but it was rather dramatic all the same, and exactly like a picture. These are straws, but one could multiply them with incidents from every farm we go to. Their talk is invariably, and without so far a single exception, to the same effect—"We will never give in, and God sooner or later will see us through."

And then I see a speech of Buller's explaining that the war is being carried on by a few mercenaries and coerced men, and that it is in no sense a patriotic war. He is emphatic on this point and his audience cheer him. One realises the difficulty of getting you to understand. The breaking up of the big commandoes and the change to guerilla tactics, in which every man fights on his own account, shows in a way there is no mistaking that it is the personal wish of each man to fight out the quarrel to the last. It is just because they are so individually keen that this sort of warfare of theirs is so hard to cope with. These men are uncoerced. Spontaneously and one by one they turn out to fight us as soon as we show ourselves in their neighbourhood, and all the suffering we can inflict only serves to harden their resolution.

Yet we certainly inflict a great deal. Boer families usually average up to a dozen. They stick together, and grow up on their farms, which are of enormous extent, and which they get to love with the instinctive force of people who have never seen any other place. Love of family and love of home are their two ruling affections. The household life of a big family on a 20,000 acre farm—three and often four generations represented—is usually uninterrupted for weeks at a time by the sight of a strange face or a bit of outside news. Their lives are altogether bound up, in their serene and stolid way, with each other and with their homes. Anything that breaks up a family is felt by them more grievously than would be the case with most people; and, in the same way, anything that severs them from "the land" would be more profoundly felt too. It amounts to an entire dislocation of their ideas of life.

This must make the war at present very hard to bear. "My dear husband and child and brothers" are away fighting. One or two of them very likely killed by this time, or in Ceylon or St. Helena. "And as for the others who are still in the field, we are in constant terror of hearing the bad news, which we know, if the war continues, must some day come." So the family is quite broken up, and now the home is being destroyed and the occupants carried off, so that altogether the chances of ever renewing the old life again in the old place seem very remote indeed.

All this should be enough to break Boer hearts, and there is no doubt they feel it very much. I can recall many scenes and incidents which show that—scenes which, if you saw them out of your peaceful, natural life, you would perhaps be never able to forget. But yet, in spite of all they have to suffer, their determination remains just the same. Anything like loud lamentations or complaints are almost unheard. They rise to the occasion, and though naturally a very simple people, who express openly what they feel, they act now in this crisis with a constant composure which I have often thought most remarkable.

What supports them and keeps them going is just that spirit of patriotism which Buller denies the existence of. A patriot is a man who puts his country first thing of all. The final result of it all, "the uselessness of prolonging the struggle," and such newspaper talk as that, is not for him. There fronts him one fact, his country is invaded; and there fronts him one duty, to fight till he dies for it. This would have been a Greek's definition of the word, and it is the Boer farmer's definition. It is of course just because patriots never do count the cost, and are what the newspapers call "deaf to reason," that they sometimes bring off such astonishing results.

The Boers have now to watch a slow, implacable, methodical devastation of their country, tract by tract. Day by day they fight, and one by one they fall. Comrades and friends drop at each other's sides; sons drop by fathers, and brothers by brothers. The smoke rises in the valley, and the home is blotted out. All that makes life worth living goes, then life itself. What sterner test can a nation be put to than this? It is a torture long and slow; the agony and bloody sweat. I know well that if my own country were invaded I should, or hope I should, behave exactly as these men are doing; and as I should call it patriotism in my own case, I cannot refuse to call it the same in theirs. You see bribery and coercion are not adequate motives, and do not explain the facts; only, unfortunately, a lot of people would rather hunt up any base motive, however inadequate, than take the obvious one if it did their enemy any credit.

It is most important that the situation should be realised at home, for if it were the conduct of the war would be changed. You cannot torture and terrorise men like this into submission. Probably no system will end the war off quickly, but certainly kind, or at least fair, treatment is the best chance and best policy in every way. The present system hardens these men's resolution to iron, and so tends to prolong the war; and it embitters Dutch hatred of the British, and so tends to perpetuate the ill effects of the war. In fact, I am convinced that it is the worst policy you could possibly adopt, and the sooner you change it the better.

As for the fighting itself, you must make great allowance for our difficulties. So long as we had big commandoes with guns, convoys, &c., to deal with, there was a definite object to hit at. It was possible to deal a blow that took effect. Now we are fighting shadows. Our columns march through the country and see no enemy, or at most only a few small parties hovering on the sky-line. Scouts and patrols are often engaged, and no one can wander out of sight of the column but the ugly voice of a Mauser will warn him back. Invisible eyes watch us all the time, ready to take advantage of detached parties or unprotected convoys. We are teased and annoyed, but never definitely engaged. We are like the traveller and the gnats—

Nor could my weak arm disperse
The host of insects gathered round my head,
And ever with me as I walked along.

Carried on in a country like this, where a man on horseback is like a bird in the air, and by people so individually keen as the Boers, the present kind of war may go on indefinitely. After all, it is the sort of war the Boers understand best. The big-battle war is a matter of science which he had in a great measure to be instructed in, but this is a war which the natural independence of his own character and self-reliant habits make natural to him. The war, now that it has become a matter of individuals, is exciting all its old enthusiasm again, and the Burghers are up in arms in every district in the country. Fighting in their own country, the Boers have one advantage over us, which is their salvation: they can disperse in flight, but we cannot disperse in pursuit.

This vagrant form of war is more formidable than it sounds. These wandering bands can unite with great rapidity and deal when least expected a rapid blow. As we cannot catch them we must be prepared to receive them at all points. The veldt is a void to us, all darkness, and it hides a threat which, as it may fall anywhere, must be guarded against everywhere. This, what with all our garrisons and enormous lines of communication, means that the far greater part of our army has to act on the defensive; to sit still waiting for an enemy who may be a hundred miles off or behind the next hill. As for our wandering columns, they have about as much chance of catching Boers on the *veldt* as a Lord Mayor's procession would have of catching a highwayman on Hounslow Heath. The enemy are watching us now from a rise a few miles away, waiting for our next move, and probably discussing some devilry or other they are up to. The line of our march is blotted out already. Where we camp one day they camp the next. They are all round and about us like water round a ship, parting before our bows and reuniting round our stern. Our passage makes no impression and leaves no visible trace. It does amuse me to read the speeches and papers in England with their talk of what we are to do with the country now we have conquered it. "With the conclusion of the war in South Africa arises the question," &c., &c. It reminds one of a child's game of make-believe. There is the same pompous air of reality. "This is the shop and you are the shopwoman. Good morning, Mrs. Snooks, I have come to buy a pound of sugar." Unfortunately the facts remain. I find that some of the shrewdest onlookers out here are just beginning to feel a sort of half doubt whether we shall ever conquer the country at all. It depends on whether the home Government and press give up their babyish "let's pretend" attitude and face the difficulties of the situation.

All this is very sad and lugubrious, is it not? and I daresay you think me a croaker; but there is a melancholy satisfaction in trying to see things as they are, and I believe what I have told you is nearer the truth than what you get from the papers. I only hope I may turn out to be wrong.

I add a note (January 12th) from Ventersberg, where we have just arrived. This has been our last trek, we believe.

Rimington takes command of his regiment, and the corps, like the rest of the Colonial Division, will be paid off. I have a vision of a great blue steamer with a bow like a cliff bursting her way through the seas on her homeward voyage. And yet I can scarcely believe it.

Bad news waits us here. They say the Colony is rising. Now mark my words. If we don't watch it, we shall end by bringing about the very state of things we have been dreading. There will be a Dutch South African conspiracy, but it will be one of our own making. We shall have our own treatment of these people to thank for it. Be sure of this, that for every house up here that is destroyed, three or four in the south are slowly rousing to arms.

You will think, I daresay, that I have been putting the case one-sidedly. Possibly that is so; but I am putting the side that wants putting. I am constantly seeing it stated that any measures are justifiable so long as they are likely to end the war. "Well, but we must end it somehow," is a common phrase. That is all rubbish. We must fight fairly, that's the first rule of all. I daresay there may have been individual acts of cruelty or treachery on the part of the Boers, but I am sure that any just and unprejudiced officer will tell you that on the whole they have behaved surprisingly well, and in a way that is really very striking when we consider how undisciplined and individually independent they are. Let us then, on our side, play the game fairly. No doubt it is very exasperating to have the thing dragging on in the way it is doing, and the present intangible, elusive warfare is desperately irritating, but there is after all nothing unfair about these tactics of the Boers, nothing illegitimate in any way; they are merely the turning to account of natural advantages; and this being the case, we have no right to lose our tempers and get vicious just because we have taken on a tougher job than we thought for. Unluckily there seems to be a big party who are prepared to do anything and fight anyhow to get the thing finished. You will gain nothing by those means. You will not hasten the end of the war, and you will make its after effects more lasting and hard to deal with.[2]

2: Here is a telegram copied from the Evening Standard of October 16, 1901. "Addressing the volunteers who have returned from the front, the Governor of Natal this morning said that he could not now refer to the Boers as dogs of war, but rather as yelping, snarling curs." As against that take the opinion of Lord Cranborne who has just come back from the front: "They had fought and they were fighting with some of the bravest, some of the most tenacious, and some of the most admirable troops that the nation had ever had to encounter;" and he ends his speech: "Personally he had, as one who had served as a soldier in South Africa, a great admiration for the Boers themselves." What I submit is, that it makes the whole difference to your chances of a settlement whether you speak of and regard your enemy as brave and admirable, or as a yelping cur. We shall have to settle down with these people sooner or later, and every paltry insult uttered and countenanced against them only makes the process much more difficult. The odd thing is that even in England they seem to excite no surprise or dissent. They are printed as a natural comment on the situation. What I always feel is, now as when I was out there, that the chances of a future agreement would be very much improved if the English people were to treat the Boers in the way that brave enemies ought to be treated, with a certain amount of courtesy and respect.

Plain Mister!

Cape Town

R. Caton Woodville.

Plain Mister!
Cape Town

I am trying to din the fact into my head that I am a civilian again and not a soldier any more. It is difficult. I find myself looking questioningly at my suit of grey flannel. It feels like a disguise. No soldiers' hands as I pass them rise in salute now, though my own involuntarily half rises in answer They look at me and take no notice. A recruiting sergeant tried to induce me this morning to join an irregular corps. He told me I should get five shillings a day, and that it was a fine life and a beautiful country.

And yet I know that, in a few days even, the civilian life that seems so unreal now will be the real, and the old soldier life the unreal. I shall not in my walks find my eyes wandering "with a vague surmise" over the nearest hilltops in search of Boers, nor measuring unconsciously the range from the top of Table Mountain, which I find myself doing even as I write this, looking up at it through the window. The trekking, the fighting, the croak of the invisible rifle, the glare of the sun, the row of swarthy determined faces, the roar of horse hoofs, all this, and the lounging days by river banks (shooting guinea-fowl and springbuck), will drop back and be shut off from one's life to rise now and then, I suppose, with the creeping of an old excitement in one's memory.

There was a heavy gloom on the last days of my soldiering. It was at Naauwpoort that I first joined the Guides. We stopped there coming down. There was the waiting-room, the very table I had slept on; the sun-baked flat where first I met the Major; the slopes where our tents were pitched—Lord! how the sight of the place brings it all back, and how different everything has turned out from what we expected; it was there that I joined, and it was there, travelling down with our time-expired men, that we first heard the news of the Queen's death. You at home will feel this deeply—of course every one must—but I can't help thinking that out here, far away from home and fighting, one feels it even more. I am almost surprised at minding so much. There is an irksome sense at the back of one's mind, even when one is thinking of other things—of loss, of something wanting. England seems less England to me than it did and I less of an Englishman. It gives a faint satisfaction to have been one of her soldiers at the end.

I will spare you my raptures on reaching Cape Town and seeing the woods and clear streams and sea again. The change from a comparatively barren country to the richly-wooded slopes under Table Mountain, and the burst of sparkling sea beyond is quite sudden. At one step, in the twinkling of an eye, you pass from monotony and desolation and the old life of the veldt into everything that is most lovely and suggestive of freedom and variety. Huge Table Mountain rises high over the town, its steep slopes wooded with forests of pine and oak. Gorge-like narrow passages wind into the upright precipices of rock and separate them into great pinnacles of grey stone. I clambered up there a few days ago, through hot-smelling pine woods, heaths of all sorts, evergreens and flowers, clear water like Scotch burns coming down among the rocks with its toss of white froth and amber pools, and such a view, when one got to the top, down over the whispering woods and out over the flat sea!

The sea was the thing that beat all—"the great sea perfect as a flower,"—the sight of it was a stab. There are great four-masted barques and full-rigged ships lying at the wharfs and outside—double t'gallant yarders, my boy; I yelled at them by way of greeting down across the tree-tops.

Nearer in lies a long black steamer, a transport. She is an ugly looking old tub, but in my eyes perfect. Handsome is as handsome does. She takes us home tomorrow, my pony and me.

LEONAUR
ALSO FROM LEONAUR
AVAILABLE IN SOFTCOVER OR HARDCOVER WITH DUST JACKET

EW2 EYEWITNESS TO WAR SERIES
CAPTAIN OF THE 95th (Rifles) *by Jonathan Leach*

An officer of Wellington's Sharpshooters during the
Peninsular, South of France and Waterloo Campaigns
of the Napoleonic Wars.

SOFTCOVER : **ISBN 1-84677-001-7**
HARDCOVER : **ISBN 1-84677-016-5**

WFI THE WARFARE FICTION SERIES
NAPOLEONIC WAR STORIES
by Sir Arthur Quiller-Couch

Tales of soldiers, spies, battles & Sieges from the
Peninsular & Waterloo campaigns

SOFTCOVER : **ISBN 1-84677-003-3**
HARDCOVER : **ISBN 1-84677-014-9**

EWI EYEWITNESS TO WAR SERIES
RIFLEMAN COSTELLO *by Edward Costello*

The adventures of a soldier of the 95th (Rifles) in the
Peninsular & Waterloo Campaigns of the Napoleonic wars.

SOFTCOVER : **ISBN 1-84677-000-9**
HARDCOVER : **ISBN 1-84677-018-1**

MCI THE MILITARY COMMANDERS SERIES
**JOURNALS OF ROBERT ROGERS OF THE
RANGERS** *by Robert Rogers*

The exploits of Rogers & the Rangers in his own words
during 1755-1761 in the French & Indian War.

SOFTCOVER : **ISBN 1-84677-002-5**
HARDCOVER : **ISBN 1-84677-010-6**

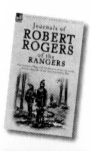

AVAILABLE ONLINE AT
www.leonaur.com
AND OTHER GOOD BOOK STORES

LEONAUR

ALSO FROM LEONAUR
AVAILABLE IN SOFTCOVER OR HARDCOVER WITH DUST JACKET

RGW1 RECOLLECTIONS OF THE GREAT WAR 1914 - 18
STEEL CHARIOTS IN THE DESERT *by S. C. Rolls*

The first world war experiences of a Rolls Royce armoured car driver with the Duke of Westminster in Libya and in Arabia with T.E. Lawrence.

SOFTCOVER : **ISBN 1-84677-005-X**
HARDCOVER : **ISBN 1-84677-019-X**

RGW2 RECOLLECTIONS OF THE GREAT WAR 1914 - 18
WITH THE IMPERIAL CAMEL CORPS IN THE GREAT WAR *by Geoffrey Inchbald*

The story of a serving officer with the British 2nd battalion against the Senussi and during the Palestine campaign.

SOFTCOVER : **ISBN 1-84677-007-6**
HARDCOVER : **ISBN 1-84677-012-2**

EW3 EYEWITNESS TO WAR SERIES
THE KHAKEE RESSALAH
by Robert Henry Wallace Dunlop

Service & adventure with the Meerut Volunteer Horse During the Indian Mutiny 1857-1858.

SOFTCOVER : **ISBN 1-84677-009-2**
HARDCOVER : **ISBN 1-84677-017-3**

WF1 THE WARFARE FICTION SERIES
NAPOLEONIC WAR STORIES
by Sir Arthur Quiller-Couch

Tales of soldiers, spies, battles & Sieges from the Peninsular & Waterloo campaigns

SOFTCOVER : **ISBN 1-84677-003-3**
HARDCOVER : **ISBN 1-84677-014-9**

AVAILABLE ONLINE AT
www.leonaur.com
AND OTHER GOOD BOOK STORES

LEONAUR

CLASSIC SF FROM LEONAUR
AVAILABLE IN SOFTCOVER OR HARDCOVER WITH DUST JACKET

SF1 CLASSIC SCIENCE FICTION SERIES
BEFORE ADAM & Other Stories
by Jack London

Volume 1 of The Collected Science Fiction & Fantasy of Jack London.

SOFTCOVER : **ISBN 1-84677-008-4**
HARDCOVER : **ISBN 1-84677-015-7**

Contains the complete novel Before Adam plus shorter works: The Scarlet Plague, A Relic of the Pliocene, When the World Was Young, The Red One, Planchette, A Thousand Deaths, Goliah, A Curious Fragment and The Rejuvenation of Major Rathbone

SF2 CLASSIC SCIENCE FICTION SERIES
THE IRON HEEL & Other Stories
by Jack London

Volume 2 of The Collected Science Fiction & Fantasy of Jack London.

SOFTCOVER : **ISBN 1-84677-004-1**
HARDCOVER : **ISBN 1-84677-011-4**

Contains the complete novel The Iron Heel plus shorter works: The Enemy of All the World, The Shadow and the Flash, The Strength of the Strong, The Unparalleled Invasion and The Dream of Debs

SF3 CLASSIC SCIENCE FICTION SERIES
THE STAR ROVER & Other Stories
by Jack London

Volume 3 of The Collected Science Fiction & Fantasy of Jack London.

SOFTCOVER : **ISBN 1-84677-006-8**
HARDCOVER : **ISBN 1-84677-013-0**

Contains the complete novel The Star Rover plus shorter works: The Minions of Midas, The Eternity of Forms and The Man With the Gash

Printed in the United Kingdom
by Lightning Source UK Ltd.
121685UK00001B/278/A